WINNING
the
Innovation
Game

By Denis E. Waitley
Seeds of Greatness
The Double Win

By Denis E. Waitley and Robert B. Tucker
Winning the Innovation Game

Denis E. Waitley
Robert B. Tucker

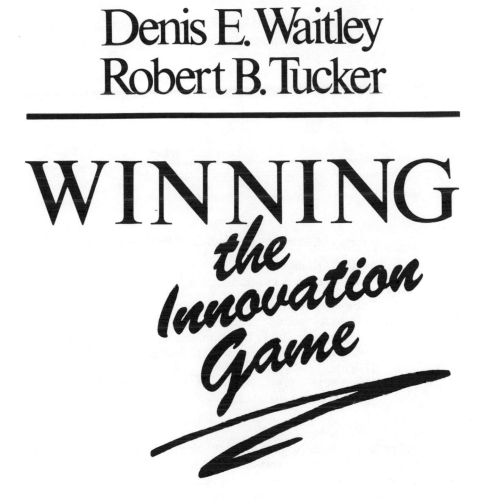

WINNING
the
Innovation
Game

Fleming H. Revell Company
Old Tappan, New Jersey

Library of Congress Cataloging in Publication Data

Waitley, Denis.
   Winning the innovation game.

   Bibliography: p.
   Includes index.
   1. Creative ability in business. 2. Success in
business. 3. Entrepreneur. I. Tucker, Robert B.
II. Title.
HD53.W35   1986   650.1   86-17879
ISBN 0-8007-1494-6

Copyright © 1986 by Denis E. Waitley and Robert B. Tucker
Published by Fleming H. Revell Company
Old Tappan, New Jersey 07675
Printed in the United States of America
All Rights Reserved

Contents

5

CONTENTS

PART II
THINKING LIKE AN INNOVATOR

PART III
IMPLEMENTING YOUR INNOVATIONS

CONTENTS

TO My Parents
Charles
and
Betty Joe Tucker

and

TO those who dare to act on their
dreams

Acknowledgments

Behind every book there is a story. The story of *Winning the Innovation Game* spans many miles and includes many lives. One builds up a considerable indebtedness that way, especially when the people one is seeking out are asked to reveal their secrets.

Through these past two years of research and writing, we have had the great fortune to spend time with some of America's most creative and capable individuals. Though we spoke with far more people than can be acknowledged here, they will recognize their contributions to our thinking throughout this book. Without their cooperation and willingness to share, *Winning the Innovation Game* would not have been possible. To each of you, then, our profound gratitude.

Writing a book is a team effort. We were fortunate to have had the wisdom, advice, insights, and feedback of some very caring and devoted teammates. Jesse Berst, Daniel Boone, Carolyn McQuay, and Colonel Bart Tucker (USAF) all read numerous drafts of the manuscript and made many valuable suggestions. All fortified us with a sense of the mission we were on, blasted faulty thinking, and occasionally tempered euphoria with further suggestions. A number of people read and commented on portions of the manuscript: Bill Bruns, Brenda Blackman, Tim McQuay, Julie Shaull, and Leland Russell.

Leland Russell, one of the innovators you will read about in these pages, gave us our title. As we were interviewing him one evening early in the project, we asked what he had in common with the other individuals we were speaking to around the country. Without hesitation he said, "We're all winning the same game—the Innovation Game." It was an "aha!" moment that needed no elaboration. Thanks, Leland.

Donna Colabella transcribed the thousands of pages of interviews upon which this book is based. Innovators never sit still. As a result, many of those interviews were conducted in taxis, on airplanes, in noisy restaurants, on busy sidewalks, and even, once, in a helicopter. Through it all—nights, weekends—Donna pressed on and we owe her our sincere thanks for her commitment to excellence.

Lisa Schmid spent countless hours at the word processor and in the UCLA library on behalf of *Winning the Innovation Game.* Her information-gathering skills and insights during the formative stages were particularly helpful. Lee Gedeiko, Mark Gunther, Shannon Williams, and Karol Petrosky all helped with research and logistical support.

To all the dedicated teammates of the innovators we interviewed—the secretaries, administrative assistants, and public relations chiefs—who helped us by facilitating our visits, we owe special thanks. One of them, Anne Manning of Federal Express, cannot go without specific mention. Anne was an early believer in this project and championed our unending requests for information and interviews when it might have been easier to have told us to get lost. Thank you, Anne, for all you did, and especially for staying up to lead us on the postmidnight Superhub Tour (her third that month) after a particularly hectic week in Memphis.

Rinaldo and Lalla Brutoco (*see* Special Acknowledgment)

did more than put us up during numerous trips to the San Francisco/Silicon Valley area. They lived the book right along with us from its inception, and their spacious Hillsborough home became a sort of innovation institute. Mr. and Mrs. Clarence Dodge graciously hosted us while we were conducting interviews in the Washington, D.C., area, as did Joseph Opiela in Boston.

Thanks also to our friend John Naisbitt. His insights into how America is changing and where it is headed influenced us profoundly. In many ways, this volume is our attempt to answer the questions raised by his book *Megatrends:* questions such as, "What do these changes mean to me as an individual? And what can I do about them?"

Special Acknowledgment: Rinaldo S. Brutoco

This book grew out of a series of conversations and days of private meetings with Rinaldo S. Brutoco, an entrepreneur, "knowledge merchant," and consultant of the first order. Together we analyzed the current culture, the nature of innovation, and the reasons some people are "winning the game" while so many others are being lost in the turbulence of dynamic change. In a sense, he has been the intellectual patron of this project.

During this ongoing dialogue, Rinaldo contributed inspiration, energy, his network of innovators, and a wealth of personal experience to the development of this book.

Rinaldo is an innovative thinker and problem solver par excellence. His real-world experiences as a chief executive officer and consultant in the television, consumer electronics, financial services, real estate, and motion picture industries allowed us the invaluable opportunity to "reality test" our concepts as we went along. Most important, Rinaldo fully incorporates in his life the principles about which we have written. His life provides proof positive that the principles of innovation work.

For ourselves, and for all of those who will benefit from reading this book, we extend our sincere and heartfelt thanks.

Introduction

The Innovation Game is not a pastime. It is the serious and studied commitment to create the kind of lives we want to live. For those willing to play it, it is exhilarating. It is the way in which certain people in America today are turning dreams into reality.

The desire for success never really changes. What does change is the route to the top: the strategies, skills, and principles winners use to gain life's rewards. This book has a simple premise: The rules of the success game have changed. Innovators have learned how to win big under the new rules. In the chapters that follow, we will show you how and why innovators thrive and prosper in this new era of accelerating change, exploding complexity, and rising competition.

This book is based upon hours and hours of exclusive, behind-the-scenes interviews with some of America's leading millionaires, entrepreneurs, educators, "knowledge merchants," corporate chairpersons, and leaders—men and women on the leading edge of their respective fields. The authors—a noted writer and a leading authority on high-level performance, crisscrossed the United States to talk to this nation's most successful innovators.

In seeking their cooperation, we let it be known that we did not want to talk about their net worth, their fancy cars, their yachts, or their vacation homes (although most of them can afford these things). We didn't ask about the trappings of success; instead we asked, "How did you get there in the first place? How do you do what you do?"

Winning the Innovation Game is based on their experiences, but it is really about you. We discovered that America's innovators have mastered a new process—a process you can learn and apply to your life. We call our discovery the Secret Skills of innovation because they are so often misunderstood or attributed to luck.

Master the innovator's Secret Skills and you will have powerful tools at your disposal. At the everyday level, innovation will empower you to introduce improvements in your career, your company, and your home. At another level, innovation can help you to discover and introduce new products, services, or methods that serve the needs of others and create additional opportunities for you and your business. And at its most important level, innovation is a proven method of creating the future you want.

With this book as your guide, you will discover how to:

- Go beyond daydreaming to consistently implement ideas.
- Devise a strategy to advance to the leading edge of your profession.
- Rid yourself of the thinking ruts that stifle creativity.
- Continue your education without going to school.
- Spot trends that spell "opportunity" . . . those that spell "beware."
- Find and build a Breakthrough Idea.

You already know about *Future Shock, Megatrends,* and *The Third Wave.* Now read what to do about them. Read how some of America's most successful men and women have learned to cash in on change . . . and how you can join their ranks!

PART I

The New Era

ONE

Winners in a World of Change

**Successful innovation is a feat not of intellect,
but of will.**

**Joseph Schumpeter
Early Twentieth-Century Economist**

I t was a small item in the *Wall Street Journal* with the curious title "They Aren't Called Terminals for Nothing." A Boston-based money-management firm had installed computer terminals with stock-picking software. As a result, the firm had fired fourteen people, including two research analysts, four

19

portfolio managers, a stock trader, and a quantitative analyst. "These people were doing a good job," the firm's president said. "There were just too many of them."

In and of itself, the item was of little significance. But it was not an isolated incident. Rather it was part of a larger mosaic of changes occurring in America today.

This book is about a group of individuals who are profiting from these changes and how you can join their select number. But before we turn our attention to these winners, it will pay us to spend a moment considering some of the victims of change and the forces that brought about their downfall.

You may be in for some surprises. The world we all prepared for is not the world we will find ahead. America has entered a new era. It has been called by many names: "post industrial society"; "information society"; "computer age." By whatever name, it is a dramatic departure from the past, characterized by rapid growth in the three Cs: change, competition, and complexity. As we examine these three Cs it will become apparent why all of us must become innovators if we hope to thrive and prosper into the next century.

The C of Rapid Change

In 1970, Alvin Toffler published *Future Shock,* the first popular book about the effects of change on society. Toffler predicted that "millions of ordinary, psychologically normal people will face an abrupt collision with the future ... many of them will find it increasingly painful to keep up with the incessant demand for change that characterizes our time."

For millions of Americans the future has arrived too soon. A giant tidal wave of change has swept over their lives, taking them not *toward* their dreams but setting them back, sometimes tragically. The victims of this Wave are not hard to find:

They are the 5.1 million Americans who lost their jobs due to "structural" changes in the economy between 1979 and 1984. They include 334,000 steel and autoworkers, 401,000 construction workers, 396,000 machinery workers, 212,000 apparel and textile workers. They include the million-plus homeless men and women in our cities, the multitudes of farmers who face foreclosure, the hundreds of thousands of petroleum industry workers displaced by plummeting oil prices, the untold numbers of divorced middle-aged housewives and mothers who must face the job market for the first time with few marketable skills.

Today's rapid changes are not confined to any particular occupational group. They are rampant within the service sector as well as the industrial sector, the sunrise industries as well as the sunset industries. They affect not only steelworkers and autoworkers but also the executives and managers of some of America's largest corporations. One of them is Ted Peterson.

A forty-nine-year-old cost accountant at AT&T's Indianapolis telephone manufacturing plant, Peterson's job was to monitor labor and material expenses. It was the only job he had ever held. His brother and his friends all worked at the plant. As he tells it, "Everybody knew everybody; everybody had worked there for years. It was like one big happy family." He had always assumed he would retire at AT&T. Although it wasn't written in employment manuals, it was generally understood that members of "the family" were guaranteed lifetime employment.

But in 1982, lifetime employment security disappeared with a lightning jolt. In January of that year AT&T agreed to settle the government's antitrust suit by spinning off regional phone operations into independent units. The divestiture was designed to encourage competition. It had that effect. An onslaught of mostly foreign manufacturers quickly flooded the market with cheaper phones. The competition hit the huge Indianapolis plant hard; demand plummeted 60 percent. In September 1983, AT&T officials announced that the facility would be shut down permanently.

Peterson was shocked. What to do next? Other AT&T facilities in the Indianapolis area weren't hiring cost accountants, especially those who, like Peterson, lacked computer skills. He didn't want to uproot his wife and two teenage children, and he was only seven thousand dollars away from paying off his suburban home. Besides, selling when so many other employees' homes were on the market would diminish its price. In his indecision, Peterson turned down a company offer to transfer to Louisiana, then later changed his mind after it was too late.

Peterson watched as hundreds of fellow employees departed, some for early retirement, some to other AT&T facilities, some to other companies. His indecision turned into defiance: He decided to stay until they made him go. His holdout worked— all the way through 1984 and halfway through 1985. Then one day his supervisor came around to his desk and unceremoniously handed him a piece of paper. On it was the announcement that July 12, 1985, would be his last day. "He wished me luck and shook my hand," Peterson recalled. "Nobody really discussed it. Everybody was too upset to talk about it."

The $58,600 severance pay Peterson received helped take care of his family's physical needs, but not his emotional trauma. Peterson considers himself lucky; he found work as a bookkeeper in an Indianapolis appliance store. But it is a far cry from the accounting job he was forced to leave. His salary there was $32,000 plus full benefits. His new salary is $14,000, with no benefits.

Ted Peterson is hardly alone. Rapid economic changes are

affecting all of us in some way. Deregulation, foreign competition, mergers, hostile takeovers, acquisitions, consolidations, restructurings, and a frenzy of cost cutting and staff reductions have already touched millions of lives.

When the rules of the game change rapidly, the Ted Petersons of this world get hit. They become victims of change, immobilized, unable even to react. Among people who lose their jobs, divorce rates escalate; drug and alcohol abuse increases.

Displacement is not just a blue-collar phenomenon. It is a pink-collar, a white-collar, and a gold-collar phenomenon as well. During the most recent recession, at least half a million white-collar jobs were lost. And despite three years of economic expansion and near-record employment levels, major corporations are still in a staff-reduction mode. Economists and labor experts predict major dislocation in the service sector through the 1990s.

In the 1970s, the U.S. economy created 20 million new jobs, but virtually none were created by the 500 largest companies. Between 1980 and 1985, the nation's 500 largest companies reduced their ranks by 2.2 million people. The message is clear: If you work for a large company, prepare for further fallout. Ford and General Motors have announced their intentions to reduce white-collar employment by a total of 20 percent by 1990. Eastman Kodak has reduced its work force by 24,000 since 1983, and Exxon by 36,000 since 1981. According to the Bureau of Labor Statistics, there is a one-in-ten chance you will be displaced this year.

"There is no longer any job security in the large companies," comments David Birch, an economist at the Massachusetts Institute of Technology (MIT). "In fact, job change in the larger companies is now much more erratic than job change in the smaller, entrepreneurial companies." As Birch's ground-

23

breaking research into job creation has shown, it is the smaller, rapidly growing entrepreneurial companies that are creating the most new jobs.

As dramatic as these economic events are, the first *C* is hardly confined to our work lives. Research by the Census Bureau shows that adults today undergo at least twice as many important "life changes" as their parents and grandparents. The bureau's surveys show that at one time, the typical American passed through five major life-cycle transitions: childhood, marriage, childbirth, child rearing, and the eventual dissolution of the marriage, usually through the death of a spouse.

Today the typical person will have at least twice that many life transitions. Among those added include: a foreshortened period of childhood innocence, a period of independent living before marriage, divorce, remarriage, and so forth. With divorce ending one out of two marriages, and with the two-income family increasingly the rule rather than the exception, the loss of childhood innocence may be the biggest change of all.

As one Census Bureau survey pointed out, "Once a stable foundation for life, childhood is now apt to be a time of drastic change as youngsters experience the trauma of their parents' separation and divorce, and the formation of blended families. All such changes have contributed greatly to the increased complexities of passing through the family life cycle."

> *Change of all types—economic, social, cultural, technological, and political—is occurring at an increasing rate. In some areas, it is not merely accelerating but exploding. The rapid rate of change shows no sign of slowing in our lifetime.*

Rapid change, while pervading every realm of our lives, is only one of the "three *C*s" that define the era we have entered.

24

The *C* of Competition

Today, competition takes place on a global scale. The smokestacks of industrial America are rusting as foreign competitors come to dominate industry after industry, from machine tools to motorcycles, from consumer electronics to steel. This onslaught threatens industries that were only recently considered America's bright hope for the future: industrial robots, fiber optics, biotechnology, even personal computers and semiconductors.

Japan took aim at the U.S. semiconductor industry in 1985. Chips that sold for $25 at the beginning of that year sold for only $3 by year's end, an 88 percent plunge. Result: The five leading U.S. chipmakers posted losses totaling $343 million. The year before they had profits of $1.3 billion.

We often fail to make the connection between rising competition and America's declining standard of living. Between 1973 and 1983, average family income of Americans in the twenty-five to thirty-four age group plummeted 17 percent, according to the Census Bureau, even though there were often two wage earners where before a family lived on one salary. Median income of men aged twenty-five to thirty-four nose-dived 26 percent. Economists like Harvard's Michael Porter and MIT's Lester Thurow attribute these declines to America's lack of competitiveness in the international marketplace. "The industries that pay the highest wages, and thus help narrow inequalities in income," Thurow notes, "are suffering the most from our lack of competitiveness." He adds that the percentage of middle-income households is declining within every age group.

The outcome of this economic reshuffling is anything but clear. What is clear is the force behind this competition: It is the inexorable yearning of people around the world to improve

25

their own standard of living. They too desire the goods and services of the material culture: the vacations, the fine homes, the cars. They too want in on the game!

Competition for a higher standard of living and quality of life has now reached global proportions—more evidence of the need for us all to reshape our thinking and skills.

Change and competition are pervasive today. And there is yet another *C* that challenges our assumptions about the way the world works.

The *C* of Rising Complexity

The third deep-seated characteristic of the new era is the increasing complexity of almost everything we do. Whether buying a home or investing our money, setting up a business meeting or learning to operate a computer, an annoying amount of complexity confronts us. There are forms to fill out, experts to consult, second opinions to solicit, seminars to attend.

Consider the impact of the computer. Designed as a tool for *managing* complexity, it also *adds* complexity, just as more freeways bring on more cars. The computer enables more rapid sorting, storing, and retrieval of data. The faster data can be analyzed, the faster decisions can be reached, and the greater the pressure to reach those decisions. The added efficiency brought on by the computer is not lost on our competitors, who in turn install computers and up the ante. The competitive edge, then, must come from better utilization of the computer, and from wringing even greater productivity out of each individual. The result of just such "laborsaving" technology is not only an increase in productivity but an expansion of complexity as well.

The proliferation of complexity is causing an increase in the amount of time we spend at work. According to a nationwide survey by Louis Harris and Associates, the work week of the typical American has been climbing steadily—from 40.6 hours in 1973 to 47.3 hours in 1984. Meanwhile, Harris reports, the average American has less leisure time today than a decade ago: 18.1 hours per week in 1984, compared with 24.3 hours in 1975. (Harris defined leisure as totally free time, as distinguished from preparing for work, commuting, doing chores, attending classes, and so forth.)

Although more people today find challenge and fulfillment in their work (and thus want to work longer hours), Harris believes the information explosion is part of the reason behind dwindling leisure time. "People have to work longer to keep up with all of the intelligence that keeps popping out of the computers," says Harris. And despite the new "work is more fun than fun" theme of the 1980s, most Americans, if they felt they could, would choose to work fewer hours in order to balance time with family, and to pursue avocational interests.

Thanks to the three Cs of rapid Change, rising Competition, and mounting Complexity, old ways of operating no longer guarantee success. As a result, each of us faces a choice: whether to stand idly by and become the Wave's next victim, or to rise to the challenge of the new era.

Innovators: Wave Riders

We spent the first section of this chapter discussing the victims of change. Now let's turn our attention to the winners. A small cadre of Americans has risen to the challenge of the new era and mastered its rules. They are the innovators. To understand how these individuals succeed where others fail, we must first define them and discover what sets them apart.

Speak with those who have suffered from rapid change and

27

you find a common theme: They dislike what is happening. They feel threatened by the new technology, by rising complexity, by the turbulent economy, and by the fierce competition. They long for the "good old days."

But speak with innovators and you come away with a strikingly different feeling. They welcome change. They are excited about the opportunities it brings. And they are optimistic about the future. For them, these are the "good new days."

Why are innovators thriving and prospering?

1. They welcome change rather than trying to resist it.
2. They have learned how to make change work *for* them rather than *against* them.
3. They have developed a unique set of skills which enables them to create opportunities.

There's nothing mysterious about why innovators benefit from change. They are creating some of it themselves. Like surfers, they *ride* the Wave, using its power to take them where they want to go. Rather than trying to resist change, they seek to harmonize with it.

In response to rapid change, innovators *introduce change* in the form of new products, new services, and new methods that increase efficiency, lower costs, and enhance productivity. They figure out how and why and where things are changing so they can exploit the possibilities. In response to increased competition, innovators create whole new playing fields. Instead of fighting for market share, they create new markets. They respond to global competition by figuring out what America is best at—and doing it. They know that America can compete globally not by slashing our own wage rates but by using our wits, our brains, and our creativity. And in response to increasing complexity, they keep things simple, creating businesses and services that reduce complexity for customers.

This new era is often called the "information age" because most people today are responsible for handling information as part of their jobs. We prefer to call it the Innovation Age, since it is what we do with the information that counts. Innovators create ideas that help people cope with the information explosion. This is what the independent college financial aids advisor does, or the "knowledge merchant" who develops expertise in a given subject and then distills it in the form of seminars, books, and consultations.

Because they are dealing effectively with the three Cs, innovators are in demand. Major companies may be cutting costs, but they are not cutting innovators from their ranks. Nor are nonprofit organizations and government. Whether or not they have defined it as such, they are searching for individuals who can create new opportunities.

The Innovator Defined

There is nothing new about innovators. They've been around throughout history, especially American history. They are the trailblazers, the pioneers, the popularizers, the visionaries, and the paradigm shifters. Most of all they are the risk takers and the problem solvers who have introduced the improvements that allowed us to progress from the agricultural era to the industrial and into the information era. Eli Whitney solved an obvious problem when he invented the cotton gin. Cyrus McCormick not only invented the reaper but he also created the first installment credit system and dealer network to allow his company to grow. Henry Ford perfected the assembly line along with a more reliable automobile for everyman. And so on through a long list of American folk heroes.

29

Throughout history, society's problem solvers have been generously rewarded for their efforts. No wonder that three of the wealthiest men in America are themselves innovators: Sam Walton, founder and chairman of Wal-Mart discount stores; Ross Perot, founder of Electronic Data Systems; and David Packard, co-founder of Hewlett-Packard. *Forbes* magazine's list of the four hundred wealthiest Americans is particularly instructive of the rewards of innovation. Of those named, 181 inherited their wealth. But of the remaining 219, 68 of them, or nearly one in three, built their fortunes through innovation.

Innovators are unique hybrids: They have the visionary's ability to look ahead, the inventor's ability to combine and create, and the entrepreneur's ability to sell customers. Above all, innovators have a burning desire to make their ideas manifest in the world. They are not content to imagine the future; they want to create it. Nor are they content to develop prototypes that gather dust on shelves. They want to connect their ideas with a customer group.

Let's look at some examples of contemporary innovators as we begin the process of distilling important lessons from their successes.

Fred Smith of Federal Express

In 1973, Fred Smith was twenty-eight and just back from Vietnam. He ran a family-owned aviation maintenance company in Little Rock, Arkansas, where parts sometimes arrived two days after he ordered them. Other times they failed to show up for four or five days.

To Smith, the unreliability of the airlines, which piggy-backed airfreight in their cargo hulls, represented more than an annoying inconvenience. He realized that his was not the only business at the mercy of the airlines, especially when he began to notice how often planes at the Little Rock airport

were hired, not to carry passengers but to ferry urgent packages. Smith began thinking of a small package-delivery business to alleviate the problem. In fact, he had already come up
with a similar idea for an economics paper he'd written while
an undergraduate at Yale.

Smith decided to act. Risking his entire family inheritance of
4 million dollars, Smith purchased a small fleet of jets and
began Federal Express, for parcels that "absolutely, positively"
had to be there overnight. Many people thought his idea was
unworkable, and when the Falcon jets flew the first night, it
appeared the skeptics might be right. Only six packages were
exchanged, one of them a birthday gift Smith was sending to a
friend. But from this shaky start, Federal Express created an
entirely new service industry, changed the way America con-
ducts business, and continues to lead the multibillion-dollar
overnight-delivery business.

"The people who were the big forces in the airplane business
missed the forest for the trees," Smith noted. "They were so
steeped in their own rules about how you had to operate that
they missed this entire [electronics] revolution. I knew that the
United States was going to be relying on the computer for its
economic prosperity. The electronic and computer age had to
have a specialized transportation system to support it. Just as
railroads bring coal to the steel companies and take steel to the
automobile companies, the electronics industries had to have
their specialized transportation system to keep it supplied and
supported."

Some observers use the word *visionary* to describe people
who do what Smith did. But visionaries and innovators are not
the same thing. The difference lies in the fact that the visionary
only peers into the future; he lacks the tools, the sense of timing, or the desire to successfully turn vision into reality.

31

Visionaries play an important role in society, in organizations, and businesses because they do look ahead. But they are ahead of the Wave. While innovators have vision, they must do something with it. They seek to translate vision into reality, and they have the drive and persistence to do just that. They are not interested in having their ideas discovered after they are gone.

Fred Smith is an innovator because he anticipated the wave's direction and successfully created an opportunity based on an emerging need.

Jacki Sorensen of Aerobic Dancing

Innovators are different from visionaries. And not all of them are entrepreneurs, either. Sometimes they become businesspersons to get their ideas out into the world.

In 1969, Jacki Sorensen was asked to host a television exercise program for the air force base in Puerto Rico where her husband was stationed. While preparing for the show, she took Dr. Kenneth Cooper's twelve-minute running test and discovered that her years of dance training had kept her heart and lungs in top shape. Sorensen had been looking for a way to make exercise fun, and when her Aerobic Dancing television show proved popular, she realized she was into something big. Later, while living in New Jersey, she refined her dance routines and took them to a wider audience. Like Fred Smith, she faced skepticism. But Sorensen's Aerobic Dancing has gathered momentum—and converts—ever since.

Jacki Sorensen is an innovator because she created a new method of staying fit and sold a customer group on her approach. Each day, instructors teach her routines in thousands of exercise classes across the United States, Japan, and Australia.

Peter Ueberroth, Olympic Organizer

When Peter Ueberroth was appointed to organize the 1984 Olympic Games in Los Angeles, he faced a monumental task. The two prior summer games, Moscow in 1980 and Montreal in 1976, could not serve as models. The Montreal Games had cost that city millions of dollars. Political tension created by the 1980 U.S. boycott of the Moscow Games prevented Ueberroth from turning to the Russians for advice. Doubts about a Los Angeles Olympic Games ran rampant. The threat of terrorism hung over the planning. Residents worried about massive debts, gridlocked traffic, and additional smog.

Then Ueberroth began to innovate. To reduce overhead, he appealed to the spirit of volunteerism and paid only half of the employees. Ueberroth recruited business by awarding "official sponsor" status. He and his team came up with solutions for every problem. They had to—a giant clock on the wall at Olympic Headquarters in Westwood ticked off the days until July 28, 1984. But when that day arrived, the gates not only opened on time, the Games became a smashing success. Traffic snarls failed to materialize, terrorists stayed away, and the feared deficit was transformed into a $225 million surplus.

Peter Ueberroth is an innovator because he inspired and led a team of thousands of inexperienced people toward creating solutions for problems which often had few precedents.

Marva Collins, Educator

Some people become innovators whether the world is watching or not. In Chicago's South Side, most people despaired of convincing ghetto youngsters that lives of illiteracy and welfare were not inevitable. Marva Collins, a second-grade teacher at Delano Elementary School, believed it was a teacher's responsibility to help children develop character, as well as to educate them. In an era of "value free" education, she sought to instill a positive self-image and to expose youngsters to a larger world.

Her efforts were hampered by the mind-set that failure was inevitable, and that anyone who tried to make a difference was naive. The longer she taught, the more she came to believe public schools were concerned with everything *but* teaching. Learning got lost in a system that was obsessed with tests and test scores and distracted by bureaucratic minutiae. Fellow teachers shunned her because she took her cause so seriously.

In 1974, feeling that she could not be effective in that environment, Collins quit. But she had not given up on her beliefs. Instead, she founded her own school and took in students who had been rejected by public schools as retarded, truant, or troublemakers. Collins taught them how to read using the phonics method. She showed them they could understand Aesop, Shakespeare, Twain, and Tolstoy.

Collins achieved remarkable results. Students who initially could not read simple sentences were soon reading above their grade levels. Many began writing stories for the first time. As word spread and the media began seeking her out, her Westside Preparatory School grew. CBS based a television movie on her life, enabling her to move to larger quarters. And a half-million-dollar grant from the rock star Prince enabled her to open a teacher-training institute, which trains eighteen hundred teachers a year.

Marva Collins is an innovator because she steadfastly sought to serve the needs of her "customer group," second-grade students. She rejected the new method of teaching reading, which she determined did not work as well, for a discarded method called phonics. When valueless education often failed to produce responsible, self-reliant citizens, she devised her own methods. And when the existing structure sought to stifle her vision of what education could be, she set out to create her own structure.

Learning From Innovators

Because of their actions, innovators like Fred Smith, Jacki Sorensen, Peter Ueberroth, and Marva Collins are role models for the new era. Over and over again in this book, we will turn to the real-life stories of today's innovators, not because they are "success stories" but because their achievements can show us how to solve problems and create new opportunities in our own lives. They can show us how to alter our methods and generate new approaches and ideas. Because of the speed of change today, there are fewer precedents to fall back on. The "tried and true" no longer guarantees success. And "resting on your laurels" can mean getting knocked out of the game.

Above all, innovators are people who realize that change brings both threats and opportunities. Consider the videocassette recorder (VCR). To theater owners and network television executives, it represents a threat to their livelihood. The networks have seen their market share decline since the VCR was introduced. Theater owners have sold fewer tickets. To consumers, however, the device represents a positive change, for it allows a widening of viewing choices and greater control over what they watch. And for thousands of video rental shops around the country, for independent filmmakers, for instructional video producers, the VCR represents not a threat but a new frontier. Just look at how one innovator turned the VCR into a fabulous opportunity.

Stuart Karl, Video Pioneer

Stuart Karl purchased his first VCR in 1978, when few people owned one. A trade magazine publisher and an avid observer of trends, Karl noticed that video rental shops offered either movies or X-rated fare. He sensed that customers would respond to videotaped instructional material on subjects ranging from cooking to exercise to public speaking. In a complex society, people wanted information on how to do things, as was obvious from a visit to any bookstore. The instructional video offered customers another choice of how that information was delivered.

As a result, Karl started Karl Video in Newport Beach, California. Like other innovators, Karl faced skepticism, what he calls the "prejudices of those already in the business," but he persevered. Then one day in 1981, his wife suggested he do a video version of Jane Fonda's best-selling workout book. Karl convinced Fonda to do it, and the video not only became the all-time best-selling instructional video but it also established the market for instructional videos—a market now under scrutiny by Publishers Row.

Stuart Karl's story illustrates how innovators turn problems into opportunities. It also shows the difference between the innovator and the entrepreneur.

Innovators and Entrepreneurs

Innovators and entrepreneurs actually have many of the same attributes. In fact, they're often considered one and the same. But there's a difference. One important distinction is that not all innovators are entrepreneurs, as we saw with Marva Collins and Peter Ueberroth. They can be found in the public as well as the private sector.

36

They *are* similar in their obsessiveness—to the degree of un-reasonableness—and this is often their downfall when their timing is off and they're too stubborn to admit it. Both entrepreneurs and innovators march to a different drummer. They are "take charge" people who take risks in the pursuit of their ideas. Innovators, like entrepreneurs, are market-driven. They want to connect with a customer group.

But they are different in the way they see the market. The entrepreneur concerns himself primarily with existing markets and conditions. The person who opens a video rental store in the suburban shopping center is an entrepreneur. The person who, as Stuart Karl did, looks ahead and says, "I think there's a market for this new product, service, or method" is an innovator. The difference:

> *The entrepreneur finds a need and fills it. The innovator anticipates or creates a need and fills it.*

Let's look at another example of how innovators are unique hybrids of visionaries, inventors, and entrepreneurs.

Dean Kamen, Medical Technologist

When he was nineteen, Dean Kamen designed a cigar-box-sized pump to help his brother, a medical student, conduct experiments on laboratory animals. He built it in the basement workshop of his family's Long Island home. The pump worked so well that Kamen's brother showed it to a professor, who used it in his own experiments. When the professor wrote up the experiment in a medical journal, giving credit to the younger Kamen, Dean Kamen's phone began ringing with calls from scientists around the world. Soon Kamen dropped out of college to keep up with demand. Gradually, as he perfected his pumps and learned ways to make them smaller, he perceived a larger customer group that needed a small, reliable, light-weight pump. Diabetics, he realized, could use such a pump to monitor the presence of glucose in the bloodstream and inject insulin to counteract it.

When we interviewed Kamen we were struck by the way he views himself. He doesn't see himself as an inventor. Inventors, he said, are all in the universities or the laboratories of giant corporations. Kamen explained that he merely combined existing technologies: microprocessors, miniaturized motors, pin-head-sized transducers that can detect glucose, and tiny lithium batteries.

As Kamen's story illustrates, the innovator is like the inventor in his desire to create a better mousetrap. But unlike the inventor, he is not content just to *build* the mousetrap. He wants it used. And Dean Kamen also demonstrates that the innovator is not always a creator; sometimes he is a combiner.

"What I did was to put all of these enormously impressive pieces of technology together," Kamen said. "By themselves, none of them were solving people's problems. Together they help the diabetic lead a more normal life, free of having to inject himself with insulin after every meal. People don't pay for technology," he added. "They pay for the solution to a problem, or for something they enjoy."

The innovator doesn't always invent new ideas. Instead, he borrows and reconceptualizes existing ones to solve problems and create opportunities.

Understanding clearly that the innovator discovers and combines existing ideas—ideas that are potentially available to all of us—encourages us to look harder at our own environments for ideas we might combine to good effect, a process we'll cover in greater detail later.

The Innovator's Secret Skills

So far in our quest to define innovators, we have contrasted them with visionaries, entrepreneurs, and inventors, and shown how they turn the three Cs into opportunities. Now let's go a step further and describe some of the special abilities that distinguish them. William Thompson, chairman of California-based Thompson Vitamins, summed up the innovator this way: "The innovator is someone who has the capacity not just of envisioning the future in an abstract, daydreaming, fantasizing kind of way, but has the interest and the capability and the drive to actually do something about that vision."

Thompson is right on target. The two most important aspects of what the innovator does is to *create* and *implement* ideas. And creating and implementing ideas requires a unique synthesis of skills—Secret Skills.

The innovator's skills are not secret by design; they are secret by default. They remain secret to the vast majority of people because they are misunderstood, dismissed as unimportant, or considered inborn "gifts." But every day that myth is rejected as more people discover that winning in the Innovation Age requires new skills, and that we can teach ourselves these skills.

The fact is, these competencies can be learned—"wired in," as one innovator put it—by anyone sincerely wanting to get ahead. There is an unnecessary mystique surrounding the innovator. Successful innovation, rather than resulting from genius or luck, is actually a learned and learnable process. Innovators aren't born knowing how to innovate; they gain the ability through conscious, directed effort and desire, and they figure it out as they go along.

For some, this learning is intuitive and comes about through

39

experience, via the "school of hard knocks." And to be sure, experience will always be the best teacher. But what this book hopes to do is expose the process of the innovator so that you can more speedily and easily "wire in" the innovator's mode of thinking and doing and use it to create your own reality.

Here are the ten Secret Skills we identified in our research and person-to-person interviews.

1. Innovators are opportunity-oriented. What's the hidden opportunity in that problem? Where is the opportunity in that trend? How can this be made to work better? Innovators search for the unsolved problems, the market inefficiencies, and the unmet needs and wants of existing customer groups; they also search for unmet needs and wants and build new customer groups.

2. Innovators are strategists. They attempt to anticipate the future to maximize their ability to thrive and prosper in that future. They continually define and redefine their goals, and have well-developed but flexible plans to reach them.

3. Innovators "unhook" their prejudices. In their approach to problem solving and opportunity creation, they constantly attempt to rid their thinking of preconceived beliefs, biases, thinking ruts, and unchallenged assumptions.

4. Innovators are trend-spotters. Innovators monitor change—social, attitudinal, technological, and so on—so as to spot new opportunities before everyone else. But what passes for "vision" is really just a unique way of deciphering where things are headed. Innovators do this by concerning themselves with the "big picture"; they utilize every available moment to keep abreast.

5. Innovators are idea-oriented. Innovators gain an edge through the way they work with ideas. They are constantly

40

generating ideas, always on the lookout for concepts they can borrow and apply from other fields, constantly developing and experimenting with new ideas.

6. Innovators rely upon intuition. In a world that is growing ever more complex and fast-paced, innovators use their intuition as a kind of sixth sense. It helps them assess risks, read people, spot emerging patterns of change, and make complex decisions.

7. Innovators are extraordinarily persistent. They are willing to "face the heat" in pursuit of their dreams. Their passion for ideas helps them overcome what might otherwise be roadblocks, and they are long-term thinkers.

8. Innovators are resourceful. They see no walls to implementing new ideas because of their skill and persistence at gathering Strategic Information: specialized, state-of-the-art knowledge and insight. They understand the role of information in the Innovation Age.

9. Innovators are feedback-oriented. They constantly poll their customer group to determine how their product or service can be improved. Feedback acts as their "checks and balances" mechanism. It guides their decisions and helps them avoid prejudices and blind spots.

10. Innovators are superior team builders. They realize they cannot succeed alone. They either need teams to help them implement their ideas, or, if they work alone, support networks of fellow professionals, mentors, friends, and advisors.

Putting the Innovator's Skills to Work in Your Life

Becoming an innovator requires developing and deploying each of these skills. As we explore these skills and how innovators use them to win, think in terms of mastering and applying them. Consider the innovator's skills as pieces of Strategic

Information. To innovate, you must juggle each of these pieces. Initially, this juggling process must be conscious. After you get the hang of it, it will become as natural as riding a bicycle. And, the more you consciously understand this process, the better equipped you'll be to spot weaknesses in your innovation technique.

Innovation is not a panacea. It is simply a better way of playing the game, a way of consciously directing your mental processes toward creating the life you want for yourself and your family. Once embedded in your consciousness, it can be applied to every area of life—to your personal life as well as your career. It will provide you with a new way of identifying and viewing problems as situations where information and ideas are needed. It will enable you to do more with less—less time, fewer resources. Innovation is a way of "leveraging your mind."

The rules of the success game are changing. Many of the new winners are innovators. You can use innovation to improve the quality of your own life, no matter what you are now doing, no matter what you want to do in the future. Before you start on that journey, however, you will need a clear strategy, a "road map" to your destination. And that's the subject of the next chapter.

TWO

Your Winning Strategy

**If you don't know the port to which you sail,
no wind is a good one.**

Seneca

By now it is obvious: There is no security in working for organizations anymore. The only place to find real security is within yourself and in your ability to anticipate and respond to changes in your company, your profession, your region, and your industry.

Here's the good news: You don't have to be vulnerable to accelerating changes. Your quality of life need not suffer; your standard of living need not drop. Instead of waiting for change to do something *to you,* you must do something *with it.* This is how innovators win.

We have studied some of America's top innovators, and in later chapters we will detail the specifics of their success strategies. First, however, we need to lay a foundation for this information. The Secret Skills of the innovator will have more value if you have a strategy for incorporating them into your life.

In a world where change is incremental and slow, a strategy is not required. In a world of rapidly accelerating change, a strategy is essential.

Webster defines *strategy* as the art of "maneuvering forces into the most advantageous position prior to engagement with the enemy." In today's world, the enemy is complacency and resistance to change. Your strategy determines the way you *react* to unexpected circumstances, how you *respond* to opportunities, indeed, how you "make your own luck." Strategy involves mental preparation for (1) dealing with variables you *can* control (such as how hard you work) and (2) managing variables you *cannot* control (such as shifts in demand for professionals in your field).

Innovators *think strategically.* They know that flexibility is more than an abstract concept; it is a mind-set. As cats always seem to land on their feet, innovators manage to make the best of a bad situation and to take a calculated risk when conditions appear favorable.

But there is an obstacle to this flexibility: complacency.

Complacency is a difficult attitude to shake off. During the post-World War II era, America was economically invincible;

growth was virtually guaranteed. Many Americans began to value security over self-reliance. They sought security in large organizations: governments, corporations, unions. Their leaders echoed the same theme: "Don't concern yourself with the 'big picture.' No need to worry about the profitability of your company or the competitiveness of your industry. Let us take care of these matters; they're over your head."

The industrial era demanded uniformity and conformity and promised security in return. Many Americans became content to let large institutions do their thinking for them. They were encouraged to believe that job security was something only a big organization could provide. And job security was their promise. But when the rules changed, it was a bigger promise than many of them could live up to. As we saw in chapter 1, millions of Americans who bought this "security complex" have suffered as a result.

Five Steps to Success

What specific steps can you take to ensure your viability in the new era? Here are five components of a winning strategy:

1. Incorporate yourself mentally. Begin to think of *yourself* as "YOU, INC.," a company with one employee: you. Today YOU, INC., may contract its services to XYZ Corporation; tomorrow it is likely to sell its services to a different organization. Incorporating yourself mentally doesn't mean you are any less loyal to your present employer. It *does* mean that you never confuse your personal long-term interests with your employer's.

By deciding not to suffer the fate of those who have been bounced out of jobs only to find that their skills were obsolete, you begin the process of protecting yourself against this possibility. Ask yourself: *How vulnerable am I and what can I do*

45

about it? What conditions must I watch? In this fashion you become *pro*active instead of *re*active.

Just as companies must "reinvent" themselves to meet the demands of the new era, so it is with YOU, INC. Establish your own "strategic planning department." Set up your own training department and make sure your prized employee is updating his or her skills and techniques. Start your own pension plan.

So far, we've been speaking of the growing possibility that you'll be dislocated. The flip side of this coin is that *you may choose to dislocate yourself.* This is one benefit of living in an era of change. The once-derogatory label "job jumper" has virtually disappeared. Today the person who puts up with a tyrannical boss or a dead-end job does so as a matter of choice.

Many innovators who mentally incorporate themselves eventually incorporate themselves in actuality. If you are already self-employed, YOU, INC., is already part of your mental set—it has to be. You must think strategically in every decision you make since your primary concern is ensuring your viability in the marketplace. Once crucial only to the self-employed, this mind-set has now become essential to all of us.

> *Today's typical American will have five separate careers in his or her lifetime. If you are not already planning for an eventual career change, you should be.*

2. Become a lifelong learner. Not long ago, what you learned in school was all you really needed to learn. You could rely upon that knowledge for the rest of your life. This is no longer a safe assumption. Today, knowledge expands exponentially. The number of scientific papers published daily is in the hundreds. Every thirty seconds, Silicon Valley produces yet another technological innovation. The result: Your education has a shorter "shelf life."

In a world where there is so much to know, innovators have a refreshing attitude toward learning. Most of them are so busy innovating that they must absorb new ideas and knowledge on the run—they are simply too busy *doing* to spend much time in classrooms. Nevertheless, they continue to learn by teaching themselves.

Their love of learning springs from a natural curiosity. And their risk-taking nature applies to the way they learn. It leads them to dig deeper, to want to know not just "how" but "why." Their pattern of learning tends to approximate what is known in eating circles as "binging"; they become fascinated with a topic and delve into it headlong, reading all the books they can find on the subject, amassing dozens of articles, seeking out the top experts.

Despite their love of learning, innovators are not "degree strivers." Many hold advanced degrees, of course, but a surprising number of them are college dropouts: director Steven Spielberg; Mo Siegel, founder of Celestial Seasonings; Regis McKenna, the Silicon Valley marketing consultant; Steven Jobs, the founder of Apple Computer; Stuart Karl, who pioneered the instructional video and produced *Jane Fonda's Workout* video, and many others.

Dean Kamen, who invented a portable insulin pump when he was in his early twenties, sums up the innovator's attitude when he explains why he never earned a degree at Worcester Polytechnic Institute:

> I tried, but I was there for an education and they were there to sell me a diploma. I had a lot of things I needed to learn so that I could do what I wanted to do, and they had this system that they were selling me. Between trying to run my business and really learn things, I was always at odds with them trying to put all the filler in the meat. Finally I just left.

Innovators do not depend on degrees; they realize their limited value. Although a formal education can add several thousand dollars to your annual income, it does not teach you how to put your ideas into action. In fact, say some innovators, universities teach just the opposite: how to spot all the reasons an idea will fail and therefore should never be tried. While he was an undergraduate economics student at Yale, Fred Smith wrote a term paper describing the concept he would later use as the basis for Federal Express. His professor awarded him a *C,* explaining all the reasons the idea wouldn't get off the ground.

Lifelong learning doesn't mean only book knowledge. In a world where working with people is a must, it also means deepening your understanding of yourself and others. At a recent gathering of the Tarrytown 100, an organization of innovative American business leaders, a shared belief emerged from a round-table discussion: Just as each of these leaders was innovating in his or her business life, they were innovating in the other spheres of their lives as well. The group agreed that the next step in an individual's *executive* growth depends on the next step in *personal* growth. Their businesses were a mirror image of both their personal gifts and their personal limitations.

If you think you've "completed" your education (and it doesn't matter when), you are on a fast track to personal obsolescence. The most obvious arena is technology, specifically computers. By ignoring the computer today, you risk becoming the illiterate of tomorrow. This era requires that you devote a portion of your energy to learning. This may come in the form of seminars and workshops, self-guided study, books, or audio and videocassette programs.

Lifelong learning may once have been a luxury. Today it is vital to continued success.

3. Become a student of change. Lewis Lapham, editor of *Harper's Magazine*, tells the story of a New York banker who felt so out of touch with the world that he wanted to hire Lapham as his personal intelligence agent.

Every morning, the banker explained, he traveled by limousine from New Canaan, Connecticut, to his Park Avenue office. He rode a private elevator to the seventeenth floor, where he remained for the rest of the day, isolated among people of his own kind. "About interest rates and economic growth he knew a great deal," Lapham observed, "but about impending social and cultural trends he knew very little."

As the world becomes more interconnected, events outside your narrow field have an impact upon your field, your career, your family, and your pocketbook. Whatever your job, it takes place in a larger context of social, technological, political, economic, and cultural change. Navigating YOU, INC., to success requires an understanding of that world. Without that understanding, you won't be prepared to innovate; you'll only be able to react and to avoid.

Many people will tell you that it doesn't really matter how well-informed you are. "You can't do anything about it anyway," goes the refrain, "so why bother to find out about things?" Here's a newspaper editorial that sums up this attitude:

> The world is too big for us. Too much going on, too many crimes, too much violence and excitement. Try as you will, you get behind in the race, in spite of yourself. It's an incessant strain, to keep pace ... and still, you lose ground. Science empties its discoveries on you so fast that

you stagger beneath them in hopeless bewilderment. The political world is news seen so rapidly you're out of breath trying to keep pace with who's in and who's out. Everything is high pressure. Human nature can't endure much more!

This newspaper editorial reads as if it were written last week. But it actually appeared more than 150 years ago, on June 16, 1833, in the *Atlantic Journal*—back in "the good old days"!

How can you avoid becoming the next casualty of the "bad new days"? Take the offensive. Instead of "stewing," start "doing." Pay attention to the early warning signs of change. Look for changes in your work, your field, and your region.

You cannot innovate if your understanding of change is erroneous, incomplete, misinformed, or outdated.

4. Understand your thinking processes. When Norman Vincent Peale's book *The Power of Positive Thinking* appeared in 1952, it was one of the first popular books to address the thinking process. Peale's message was at least as old as the Bible itself, which says that "as a man thinketh in his heart, so he becomes" (*see* Proverbs 23:7). Peale showed how our thinking process makes us either winners or losers. What counts, Peale argued, is not native intelligence, social origin, or even education. It is how we direct and control and channel our thinking that ultimately shapes our self-image and our lives.

For millions of men and women, positive thinking has become part of a strategy for success. The positive-thinking movement of the 1950s paved the way for the human-potential movement of the 1960s and 1970s. Today, as both movements continue to evolve, they agree on the importance of enhancing and understanding the thinking process.

You can learn to become a positive thinker. Likewise, you can learn to become a more creative thinker, a more effective problem solver, and a better decision maker. Thinking ability, as we will demonstrate in chapter 4, has less to do with intelligence than many presume.

Why improve your thinking? One reason is that companies and organizations seek out and richly reward individuals with this skill. Haley Associates, Inc., a New York executive recruiting firm, reported a noticeable increase in companies requesting innovative thinkers. In addition to management and organizational skills, says a Haley vice-president, "Companies are looking for employees with the ability to enter the problem-solving process with a fresh mind and come out with solutions that are unique." Haley evaluates candidates' creative thinking skills on how they respond to three essential questions: Does the person look at a problem from different points of view? Does he tend to make snap judgments? Is there a sense of openness in the candidate's thinking?

Success in the new era is heavily dependent upon innovation, creativity, and the solving of problems for which there are no precedents. While new technology is often the driver of economic and social change, the high-technology sector of the economy creates relatively few new businesses or jobs. Both are created by individuals who apply technology in new ways.

If you are an executive, manager, entrepreneur, or knowledge worker, your success depends on how well you think. You are not paid to collect, sort, store, or retrieve information, although you may do these things as part of your job. You are paid to interpret that information and to create and implement new ideas.

5. Begin work on a Breakthrough Idea. You can accomplish great things if you focus on what you want to do, and then figure out how to accomplish it. We call this "finding your Breakthrough Idea."

At some point, every true innovator develops a Breakthrough Idea and turns it into an opportunity. Fred Smith's Breakthrough Idea was to start Federal Express. Marva Collins' was to start her own school. Jonas Salk's was to develop an effective polio vaccine. Many innovators work on several ideas at once. Look around at the most ambitious people you know. Everyone who is "going places" has a guiding vision. They are totally focused on making an idea happen. This mind-set has a mysterious effect. Because they are in motion (toward a goal), the changes of the world do not cause them as much distress as those who are passive observers.

You've probably already implemented a number of Breakthrough Ideas in your life. Getting a college education. Breaking into your current field. Getting married. Starting a family. Buying your first home. These events were breakthroughs because they were conceptual leaps. They required that you figure out how to do them, how to get others to go along with your idea, how to make the idea real. A Breakthrough Idea represents a stretching of your abilities, skills, and energies to make the idea manifest in the world.

Generating and implementing Breakthrough Ideas is the only way to create your own reality.

If you haven't discovered your life's work, doing so can serve as your next Breakthrough Idea. If you've already chosen a career, your next breakthrough may be to develop a new product or service for your company. Or it may be something you want to do in your spare time: an invention; a play; a book.

Whatever your breakthrough, the world has never been

more open to new ideas. This is truly an opportunity society; the barriers to entry have diminished. Capital was formerly a barrier, but now people start new businesses on shoestring budgets in garages, basements, and spare bedrooms, and go on to build them into empires. If you can come up with an idea that solves somebody's problem, makes life more convenient, simplifies some process or procedure, offers greater choice, or satisfies at a lesser price, the world really will beat a path to your door. Never have Henry David Thoreau's words been truer: "The world will step aside for the man [or woman] who knows where he wants to go."

It is never too soon to begin thinking about your next idea. The more lead time you have, the better off you'll be. The company leader cannot afford to become so narrowly focused on this year's projects that he or she fails to generate ideas for next year. The author embroiled in finishing his present book must be thinking ahead to his next one. The same holds true for YOU, INC.

> *In the Innovation Age, it's not enough to think of yourself as "just an employee." If you want to take charge of your life, you must be working on a Breakthrough Idea.*

How you can discover and develop such ideas is the major concern of this book. If you are already in the midst of making your breakthrough happen, so much the better—use this book as a guide to help you on your way. If you haven't come up with an idea that gives you a burning desire to build it into something, this book can help you find one.

One key to making breakthroughs is understanding yourself, your limitations, and your potential. In the next chapter, we'll help you take a brief personal inventory that will get you started on the road to winning the Innovation Game.

THREE

A strategy is trying to understand where you sit in today's world. Not where you wish you were or where you hoped you would be, but where you are. It's trying to understand where you want to be five years out. It's assessing the realistic chances of getting from here to there.

**John Welch, Jr.
Chairman, General Electric Company**

There are many parallels between the business strategy referred to by Welch and the strategy of YOU, INC. Both require "trying to understand where you sit in today's world."

Both require understanding your strengths and weaknesses and clearly defining where you want to go. This chapter is an inventory designed to help you do these things.

So far you've read this book for the information. But becoming an innovator isn't something you can do passively. Here's your first opportunity to take action: by writing out your responses to the questions in this inventory. The difference between merely thinking about these questions and taking the time to write out responses is the difference between, to paraphrase Mark Twain, lightning and a lightning bug. There are several advantages to committing your thoughts to paper. First, your ideas will become more focused. Second, you'll have a record for later reference. By taking this first step, everything you read henceforth will help you more.

1. Where would you really like to be in five years? If you're serious about taking control of your life, start by figuring out where you want to go. One way is to project yourself into the future as you would like it to occur.

Award-winning graphic designer Milton Glaser used to pose an exercise to his students: Design an ideal day for yourself five years from now. Where do you live? How does your day begin? What's the view over the breakfast table? What kind of work do you do? And so on through the day, filling in as many specifics as possible. Who are your friends? What events of the day give you satisfaction? What do you do just for fun?

Consider dozens of alternatives. Let your imagination go. How do you want life to work for you? Do you want love in your life? Do you want greater wealth? Do you want to be thinner, more attractive, healthier? Do you want to make a contribution to society? Do you want to break in to an entirely different career?

If you have faithfully written out a portrait of your life on that hypothetical day, you will have examined your own goals and desires in a remarkably thorough fashion. In mapping out this vision of your future, you are already improving the chances that you'll realize it. When you achieve one or more of your goals, you are creating your own reality. This is what the innovator does best.

2. How is what you are presently doing helping you build the future you really want for yourself? Certainly it is providing you with a living. But what is it doing in terms of advancing you toward where you really want to be? This question implies another question: Have you discovered your life's work? If you know what it is you really want to do, are you working to make that dream a reality? If you haven't discovered your life's work, what are you doing on a daily basis to try to find it? Even if you are reasonably satisfied now, it's still a good idea to ask yourself such questions. You cannot expect to be an innovator in a field, a job, or a career you aren't passionately interested in.

3. What is the most innovative thing you've ever accomplished? Was it to quit a job that was getting you nowhere? Or was it something positive? Maybe you quit selling safety equipment and fulfilled your ambition to become a career consultant. Maybe you went back to school and earned your degree. Maybe you created a new product or service for your company. Or maybe you organized a charity drive and raised a record amount of money.

Giving serious thought to this question will reveal what you have accomplished so far. It won't, however, indicate where you can go.

4. What is the ratio of ideas you've been able to bring to fruition versus those you've had to give up on? When you break through with an idea, you receive an invaluable form of feedback that makes it easier to act on your next idea. This feed-back includes: feelings of pride and a sense of accomplishment, "strokes" from your colleagues, friends, and family, enhanced self-worth, financial reward, and a feeling that you've found your niche in this complex world. Most important, you realize that you have figured something out that didn't exist until you came along.

Unfortunately, people who never stick with an idea long enough to turn it into a "success episode" never receive this feedback. They wander from idea to idea hoping this will be the one. We've all known people like this; it seems every time we see them they're excited about some new scheme. This week they're going after their private pilot's license; next week they've decided to go back to school in electrical engineering, and next they've decided to become screenwriters. But we never hear any more about their former "great" desires, and to bring them up seems almost impolite.

How about your own track record? What is your ratio of ideas dreamed up to ideas successfully implemented? To fully explore and come to grips with the matter, it is essential to write out your responses. For whenever you try to get others to believe in and support your idea, one question will inevitably arise: "What's your track record?" If this question knocks you off guard, you're sunk. It says that you're not in touch with your own strengths and weaknesses, a quality essential to any-one seeking to innovate. It says people shouldn't invest in you because you are an unknown entity—*even unto yourself.*

One way to approach this question is to write down five ideas you've come up with in recent years that, when you im-plemented them, either solved a problem or created an oppor-tunity. Also record the kind of feedback you received from your customer group, if any. How did implementing each idea make you feel at the time? Record the specific pleasures of having been successful.

After you've explored your successes, write down five ideas that didn't bear fruit. Here, you aren't looking at ideas that you merely thought about, but ones you attempted to implement. These were ideas you were serious about and believed you could forge into reality, and ones you launched. These might have been goals you set at the outset of the new year; ideas you came up with to expand your business; new directions you decided to take in your life. Why didn't they succeed?

If you found it was much easier to come up with ideas that didn't bear fruit than ones which did, it might mean your attempt to realize your vision is in the beginning stage. Or it could mean that your ideas are not well grounded. If many of the ideas you listed are lying around in filing cabinets, or worse, you've never even bothered to write them down, it probably means you've allowed yourself to lapse into what we call the Dreamer Mode. (We'll learn more about the various thinking modes and how to use them to our advantage later in this chapter.)

You may need to renovate your innovation process: the way you generate ideas, research, refine, and reject them, further hone and build on them, and ultimately decide to launch them. You may need to test your ideas more thoroughly before you become committed to them. You may need to think on a smaller scale and complete a smaller project so that you break out of the cycle of starting ideas and never finishing them.

All of these themes will be dealt with in subsequent chapters. For now, it is important that you begin to identify how well you have taught yourself this process of creating and implementing ideas. As you read on, try to determine whether the particular skill being discussed is one that you have mastered sufficiently, or whether it is an Achilles' heel.

5. What are your prejudices? What would you say is holding you back from achieving your goals? Are there certain excuses you use over and over? Here are a few possibilities to refresh your memory:

- I don't have what it takes.
- I don't have the education.
- I don't have the clout to break into that field.
- I don't have the talent.
- I'm too old/too young.
- I don't have the self-discipline.
- I don't want the responsibility.
- I'm trapped in my present job.
- I don't like having to sell my ideas.
- The field I'm in has gotten too competitive.
- I don't have the credibility.
- I lack the energy.
- I'm not a self-starter.
- I'm before my time.

If any of these lines seem familiar to you, it is important to realize that they are prejudices—they stand between you and achievement of your goals and ideas.

6. Figure out what thinking mode dominates your thinking. By now, you've probably realized that innovation has a great deal to do with the mental realm—specifically, with the way we train and channel our thinking. We must learn to *think* as innovators before we can *act* as innovators. And we have to *believe* in our own creativity and abilities in order to achieve the Innovator Mode.

As you read descriptions of the four thinking modes below, ask yourself this question: *How often does this mode seem to best describe the type of thinking I'm doing?*

Victim Mode: In the Victim Mode we are preoccupied with the past and with things we cannot control. Our minds are filled with self-talk about what "shoulda, coulda, mighta, wish you had" done, not what we're planning to do in the future. Our outlook is "whatever happens, happens and there's nothing I can do about it." If your job is suddenly moved offshore, you blame "the system" or "bad luck" and make no effort to understand *why*. In the Victim Mode, you are pessimistic about the future.

Sustainer Mode: In the Sustainer Mode we are preoccupied with the present: the present view of reality, the present needs of the market, the present societal prejudices. The sustainer's favorite response to new ideas is: "That's not the way we've always done things at XYZ Corporation," or the old saw, "If it ain't broke, why fix it?" If the company installs a new computer, the sustainer will learn to use it—but only enough to get by.

Sustainers do have ideas, but safe ones—the parameters are known in advance. They want guarantees: "If I do this, I'll get that in return."

Dreamer Mode: In the Dreamer Mode, we say things like: "I could have done that. That's nothing. I thought of the drive-in hamburger idea a long time ago. Ray Kroc just met the McDonald brothers and fell into it. Kroc was lucky, that's all."

Like the innovator, the dreamer is full of ideas, but he or she is unwilling to figure out the steps necessary to bring an idea to fruition. All of the dreamer's ideas have equal merit—they are all "far out." And some dreamers can talk quite a convincing game. They use buzz words, fast comebacks, and borrowed insights to get others to take them seriously. The dreamer can be found in the executive suite (the "articulate incompetent") or in the gutter on Skid Row—the higher off the ground, the smoother the rap.

Innovator Mode: In this mode, we don't merely react to change, we create some of it ourselves. Like the dreamer, the innovator constantly comes up with new ideas, but innovators take steps to turn their best ideas into realities.

We decide to operate in a particular mode by the way we program our minds (or allow them to be programmed) and by the rewards we perceive from operating in a particular mode.

7. Are you willing to take full responsibility for your life from now on? If your answer is yes, keep reading. If your answer is no, there's nothing we or anyone else can do for you to help you become an innovator.

Congratulations! You have just finished what we hope was a challenging, enlightening (maybe at times painful) self-inventory. By responding honestly to these questions, you have established more clearly where you stand, and possibly you've become aware of areas in which your thinking needs improvement.

Now you are ready to master the specific skills it takes to win the Innovation Game. One essential: the ability to see what's on the horizon. In the next chapter, we'll look at how America's top innovators spot trends in time to cash in on them.

PART II
Thinking Like an Innovator

FOUR

Where is the wisdom we have lost in knowledge?
Where is the knowledge we have lost in information?

T. S. Eliot

T he official investigation of the 1983 terrorist attack on American marine headquarters in Beirut came to a startling conclusion. The security breach was caused in part by *too much* information. Overwhelmed with warning cables and intelligence reports, the marines tragically failed to respond to accurate data.

65

Today, many people find themselves in similar situations. They feel bombarded with information. Memos and mail, publications and periodicals, beepers and buzzers clamor for their attention—so they tune out, retreat into their comfort zones, and watch the world zoom past.

While such a reaction may be understandable, tuning out is dangerous. As the marines discovered, receiving hundreds of reports about security breaches should not lull us into believing that none of the threats are real. To separate the noise and clutter from that which is valuable, you need an information strategy, and that's what this chapter is all about.

Philosopher George Santayana once said that those who do not study history are condemned to repeat it. Were he alive today, he might add that those who do not seek out the shape of the future will be deprived of its opportunities.

We are living in a time when one of the most important skills you can develop is the ability to stay abreast of change.

Trend-watching, staying abreast, information gathering, "looking out ahead"—all are collective aspects of a vitally important survival skill in the new era. Those who have the insights about change will thrive and prosper; those who have an obsolete knowledge base will suffer the consequences.

How Innovators Keep Abreast

In studying America's leading innovators, we were constantly struck by how well informed they were on a broad range of current events, issues, and trends, both within and outside of their particular fields. They had a "finger on the pulse" of a society in motion. This connectedness to the wider world enables innovators to stay slightly ahead of their time.

And what is hailed as vision is often just an intense appetite to understand what's going on.

William Thompson, chairman of California-based Thompson Vitamins, put it this way: "The people I consider innovators have such an appetite for new ideas and new information that their problem is more a time-management one. They're so open to these things that they have to discipline themselves— they're like kids in a candy shop."

Bill McGowan, the founder of MCI Telecommunications Corporation, reads four hours a day. Excessive, you say? McGowan doesn't think so. In 1982, he happened upon an article in the Stanford Business School magazine entitled, "The Skunkworks." It told about a group of Lockheed "intrapreneurs" who developed, in record time, the U-2 spy plane separately from Lockheed's regular design bureaucracy. As McGowan read, he became excited, for the article expanded and reinforced theories he'd been thinking about. Maybe the same concept would work on a unique project he had in mind. As a result, he established a "skunkworks" task force down the block and away from headquarters. The result, only nine months later, was MCI Mail, the company's electronic mail service.

"That's a very specific payoff from my reading," McGowan reports. "I'm convinced that wide reading helps you make better decisions even though you might not specifically be able to say why."

Innovators don't look at trend-watching as "one more thing I gotta do." They love it! They are dazzled by breakthroughs, interested in other people, and concerned about political issues and social problems. They believe there has never been a more exciting time to be alive!

Staying abreast is not something innovators *do* but an integral part of *who they are.* They utilize every available moment for information gathering. They take the social risk of asking questions others might consider embarrassing. Interview them and they manage to interview you as well. Talk about new ideas and their eyes light up. They have a knack for seeking out what Thompson calls "information-rich environments." They network to find people knowledgeable in subjects they want to learn more about. And they have an easygoing manner of encouraging others to talk.

Why do innovators take information gathering to such an extreme? Part of the answer is their insatiable curiosity. Another part is strategic: Innovators ride the Wave of change because they constantly study the Wave. A knack for trend-watching, which precedes trend-spotting, is one of the innovator's Secret Skills. It is one of the things innovators do to make their own luck.

Why Innovators Seem So Lucky

Remember the parable of the real estate investor who bought up the cheap swampland on the outskirts of town? Everyone told him he was crazy. Years later, when the city had grown, the man drained the land, built a shopping center, and made a fortune. His friends stopped calling him crazy.

In fact, this was what happened when investors bought into New England in the early seventies, when its textile mills were closing, and many workers were unemployed. Before long, Route 128 outside Boston became a center for high-technology companies. Today these early investors are regarded as visionaries. But like the real estate investor, they were really just people who had mastered the art of trend-watching.

Innovators know it is necessary to seek out the direction of change if you are going to spot new opportunities before everyone else has jumped on the bandwagon. That's what trend-watching is all about. It is the art of seeking the keenest possible vision of the future by observing and understanding the present.

Why is it so important to gather information and watch trends? You are the sum total of what you read, hear, see, and experience. Your understanding of the big picture is made up of hundreds of thousands of impressions and bits of information. Think of these bits as files—and your mind as a filing cabinet. Now consider what you're adding (or *not* adding) to those files: the newspaper article you read this morning; the company briefing you attended yesterday; the conversation you had last Wednesday with a colleague after the tennis match.

Unless you continuously add fresh information and insights to your files, they'll soon become outdated. Put useless information in them, and that's all you'll ever be able to take out. But feed your mind the latest information and ideas and the cumulative effects are phenomenal. People will start thinking you have that most valued attribute: vision.

The knack for successful information gathering isn't something we are born with. Like the innovator's other Secret Skills, it is one that can be developed. Here are nine steps to becoming your own trend-spotter:

1. Audit Your Information Intake

When you diet, you become conscious of your caloric intake. By monitoring your information intake, you can cut down on your consumption of mental "junk food" and start making more rewarding informational choices. Take a moment now to audit your intake by writing down the names of the newspapers, magazines, newsletters, and trade publications you currently read.

Now study your list. Do these publications provide you with the information you need to accomplish your objectives? If not, what must you add to the list?

How do you spend your nonworking hours? Are you one of the statistically average Americans who watches seven hours of television per day? Or do you use television selectively in your information diet?

Remember the banker in chapter 2 who felt so baffled by events outside his field that he wanted to hire an intelligence agent? Is *your* information intake anemic? If the media (newspapers, TV, magazines, radio) is your only source of information, your focus is too narrow. Reading must be supplemented by exchanges with informed people and with front-line observation.

Do you trade information among colleagues, co-workers, and professionals in your field and community? How valuable are these exchanges? How are you working to improve the network of friends and associates who provide you with top-quality information? If you are not satisfied that you're getting all the information you need, look now for ways to improve your information intake.

Finally, how much time per day do you spend reading? Although quality is more important than quantity, absorbing new information takes time. Our study revealed that innovators often spend as much as a third of their business day reading.

2. Revive Your Sense of Wonder

Dangle an object in front of an infant and the child will be totally absorbed in trying to understand that "information." If the object twists in the wind, the infant is amazed anew. As babies, we all had this sense of wonder. We absorbed data at a

70

phenomenal rate. Everything was new, foreign, interesting. But growing up often means growing jaded. It often means shutting down the number of avenues through which information flows to us. Innovators rebel against this "aging" process. They realize a fundamental precept:

> *What we do is determined by what we think. What we think is determined by what we experience. And what we experience is determined by what we expose ourselves to.*

3. Develop "Front Line" Observational Skills

Most of us have read a newspaper account of an event we saw firsthand, even if only a sporting event. When we read about it the next day, or saw it on television, we felt the report didn't convey the essence of what happened. And that's the point: Nobody can do your observing as well as you can. You are your own best information gatherer. It is important to draw your own conclusions and to remain active rather than passive when absorbing information.

Perhaps you've spotted a trend before the media. Perhaps you noticed an unusual number of gas stations closing in your community. Only later did you read newspaper accounts of gas station closures. If this type of connection occurs often, it's a good sign you are already a top-notch observer. If you haven't spotted such trends lately, try to consciously "tune in" to your own observations of the world around you. For example, you arrive at the airport to find your flight delayed an hour. Instead of digging into your briefcase and doing paperwork, this is an excellent time to observe. Watch the behavior of arriving and departing passengers, eavesdrop on someone's conversation, strike one up yourself, or go scan the newsstand, not necessarily reading articles but just looking at what is available.

Listening in on conversations helps expand your world view by following the thoughts of people you might not meet ordinarily. What are they concerned about? How do they see themselves? What do their values seem to be? Rather than relying on television depictions, you are developing your own "mental files" regarding the ways people really behave, think, and feel.

4. Ask Questions

You can't get all your information simply through active observation. Take the initiative to ask questions—even of perfect strangers.

Robert Hazard is president and CEO of Quality Inns International. Hazard revolutionized the lodging industry in the early 1980s with his concept of "market segmentation"—a three-tiered range of standardized rooms at various price levels, all under the Quality International umbrella. The innovation has helped the franchise, once a floundering regional also-ran, become a major contender. In a three-year period, Hazard and his team nearly tripled the number of Quality Inns from 339 to over 900 in 1986. Market segmentation has become such a hot idea that most major chains have followed Hazard's route. In 1984 alone, some fifty new hotel brand names were created, including Marriott's Courtyard and Holiday Inn's Crowne Plaza.

Hazard formed this Breakthrough Idea from front-line information gathering: interviewing a barber. While in Phoenix on business, Hazard struck up a conversation by asking, "So, where do you go on vacation?" He got an earful. In small towns, the barber stayed in moderately priced motels. He refused to pay more than twenty or twenty-five dollars a night. But when he hit the big cities—Las Vegas, San Francisco—he always stayed in style; price wasn't a consideration. By leading with questions, Hazard obtained key information—*information his formal marketing research hadn't revealed!*

" 'What do you do for your vacation?' is my favorite ice-breaker when I'm seated next to a stranger in a waiting room or on an airplane," Hazard told us when we visited Quality Inns International headquarters at Silver Spring, Maryland. "People start talking about their travel patterns, and I get an outsider's view of my industry. That kind of information is invaluable."

Hazard instinctively does what the best interviewers do. He knows that the way you interact with people determines whether you come off as nosy or fascinated, prying or respectfully interested. Hazard lets others talk and he listens. He looks for connections between what they say and what his other information sources have told him. He cross-checks his own information in such situations, but so casually that the other person doesn't perceive it as an interview at all.

Becoming a good, informal interviewer involves asking open-ended questions rather than questions which demand only a *yes* or *no* response. It involves asking neutral questions such as, "What do you think of____," rather than, "You liked____, didn't you?" Becoming a good interviewer also requires active listening: Don't be afraid to nod your head, smile, look puzzled if you're puzzled, admit you don't understand when you don't, or show enthusiasm when you're enthused.

Interviewing is one skill you may never have thought you needed—yet we get much of our information from conversations with others. If you think it might help, you could take a journalism course in basic interviewing at your local university or junior college and find out for yourself how much more you can get out of your interactions with people by knowing how to ask questions and really listen to the responses. You are already interviewing employees and colleagues all the time, so make the most of this information-gathering skill.

5. Adopt the Methods of Professional Trend-Watchers

In recent years, professional trend-spotters have multiplied rapidly. In the race to predict what will happen in the near future, they scan newspapers, conduct polls, monitor bellwether countries such as Sweden, and pore over obscure trade publications—all with the goal of seeing the earliest signals of change.

John Naisbitt, author of *Megatrends* and chairman of the Washington, D.C.-based Naisbitt Group, employs a method known as "content analysis." It is patterned after World War II intelligence-gathering methods. Allied forces discovered the strategic value of reading newspapers smuggled out of small German towns. These papers sometimes carried reports of spot shortages of food or fuel, which revealed the situation behind enemy lines. Likewise, a Swiss intelligence team figured out where German troops were massing by reading the social pages to see which generals were in what towns.

Naisbitt came upon the Breakthrough Idea of using content analysis as a trend-spotting tool in 1968. He read a book by a historian who had used the technique to study the Civil War. Impressed, Naisbitt went to a newsstand and bought up all the out-of-town newspapers. He was amazed at what they collectively revealed.

The Naisbitt Group hires researchers who scan 300 daily newspapers from Toledo to Orlando and who clip articles on local concerns. The researchers measure the articles for length, then sort them into dozens of topics such as decentralization, networking, the transformation from an industrial to an information society, and so on. By monitoring increases and decreases in the amount of print devoted to various issues, Naisbitt is able to quantify society's changing concerns and priorities. The theory behind content analysis is that change begins at the grass roots, and therefore local and regional behaviors provide a useful way of identifying social priorities.

Like the Naisbitt Group, a program at SRI International (formerly Stanford Research Institute), the Menlo Park, California, research and consulting organization, uses a form of content analysis. Its Business Intelligence Program gathers information not from domestic newspapers but from worldwide publications. SRI scientists, engineers, and management consultants in Menlo Park, Washington, D.C., London, Tokyo, Singapore, and other cities volunteer to monitor publications in their respective fields for patterns of change. They report their observations to program coordinators at SRI's headquarters, where incoming data is reviewed monthly.

By contrast, Yankelovich, Clancy and Shulman, Inc., a New York research firm, doesn't use published reports to spot emerging changes. Instead, the firm's trend-spotting is based on detailed public-opinion surveys to twenty-five hundred Americans each year. These surveys are designed to reveal changes in attitudes, values, and spending patterns.

The Strategic Information generated by this method doesn't come cheap. The *Yankelovich Monitor,* one of the company's reports, costs clients $25,000 annually.

If you can afford such services, great. If not, you can still adopt the methods of the pros. For example, you can do content analysis on your "in basket." What is in there today versus this time last year? And what about the junk mail and advertisements you receive? A little scanning before you consign them to the wastebasket can provide valuable clues as to developing trends.

Also, read the local newspapers when you're on the road and make inferences about the state of a region's economy or compare the job opportunities listed in your local newspaper with those of a year ago. SRI International's trend-spotting system can be easily adopted by anyone wanting to set up an information network. Although you can't formally interview twenty-five hundred people the way Yankelovich, Clancy and Shulman does, you can "interview" people in social situations for clues to the ways attitudes, values, and life-styles are changing.

We asked Florence Skelly, former president of Yankelovich, Skelly and White, and currently president of Telematics, Inc., for advice on becoming more adept at spotting trends. Here are her suggestions:

> Keep your eye on the popular culture. Make an analysis —look at magazines, watch television, go to the movies, watch MTV. What themes run through current movies, books, magazines, videos? What values are portrayed? Once you get a handle on what everyone is singing about, you may find popular music very instructive. What are people singing about now? Loneliness; whether love is really worth it; affiliation. You can learn a lot if you can let go of your own value judgments and really *observe*.

6. Make Your Reading Time Count

Many people don't read much. Others read only to soak up details of the latest disaster, the latest terrorist incident, the latest scandal, the latest celebrity profile, the latest trashy novel— in short, for all the wrong reasons. Innovators, on the other hand, use their reading time to infuse and inspire themselves with new ideas and information. To them, newspapers, magazines, newsletters, professional journals, and nonfiction books are helpful tools.

A University of Michigan study found that one-third of all physicians in the United States are so busy working that they are two years behind the breakthroughs in their own field. Finding reading time is a challenge, but it doesn't stop innovators from keeping up. Dr. John Marlow, head surgeon at Columbia Hospital for Women in Washington, D.C., is about as busy as one man can be. He performs five hundred surgeries a year. In many of the gynecological surgeries he performs he uses lasers as scalpels and sutures fine enough to pass through a human hair. A cinematographer as well as a surgeon, Marlow was the first physician to receive an Emmy Award, for his film footage of the human embryo on such television programs as "The Body Human." Two or three times a month he speaks to professional audiences, frequently in different parts of the country.

For Marlow, flying time becomes reading time, which is why he doesn't rely on what flight attendants might bring down the aisle. Before boarding a plane, he buys a dozen or so different magazines: business, computer, science, news, photography, and literary periodicals. He says:

> I tend to scan and read rapidly to see what is of interest. It's important for me to read the business magazines to see where the money is going in communications. Are we switching to laser discs? Will that be the next technology? If so, that means I should develop some expertise in that. Where is America heading in basic research? What's happening in Japan? I'm also interested in the military and space programs, because that's where a lot of basic research is done. For instance, some of the fiber optic research in laser surgery is in the guided-missile system. As that be-

comes declassified, we have these tools to use as surgeons. So in determining where to see the next advance, I have to look at business magazines and newspapers. My interest is at the cutting edge of technology as it applies to the practicing doctor. I want to be right where something will be applied not as a research tool but as a practical clinical tool.

To make the most of your reading time, read actively rather than passively. Look for the point the writer is trying to make. Innovators like John Marlow make the most of their reading time by sampling broadly and reading selectively. They skim over disaster stories in favor of articles that contain ideas, and these they read very slowly, stopping to take a note or two, or to jot down an idea.

Innovators read intuitively. They are looking for what's different, incongruous, new, worrisome, exciting. Through practice, they've developed the skill of making connections between seemingly unrelated events. They ask, "How does what I'm reading jibe with everything else I've heard about this issue? How will this front page item affect what's on the business page tomorrow?"

You can read intuitively by tuning in to possible patterns, making inferences: "If this is true, then maybe that is true also." Look for information that jumps out because it surprises you and challenges long-held assumptions. Look for articles reporting on new solutions to old problems, changes in people's values and life-styles, new trends in business, breakthroughs in science and technology.

In addition to sampling a broad range of publications, it is important to be open to whatever hits you. Scan everything from advertising copy to flyers, matchbook covers to billboards, always looking for the unexpected, always broadening your world view. *This* is the mind-set of the innovator.

The common assumption is that the most important news of the day is in the headlines. Often this isn't the case. Chances are that the news you can use is buried inside. The invention of the transistor, when first reported by the *New York Times,* was buried in an inside article on the electronics industry.

The most useful information in newspapers is often contained in feature articles. Feature stories report on trends, scientific and medical breakthroughs, new ideas, people sharing their ideas, and may offer "how they did it" clues and information. If your daily newspaper doesn't run features, consider reading national newspapers such as the *Wall Street Journal* or *USA Today,* or receiving an out-of-town newspaper by mail.

Here is a list of feature articles we culled from the *Los Angeles Times* during a typical one-week period:

- How acupressure is being used to help people quit smoking
- A highly successful private adult education school called The Learning Tree
- Tom Peters' Skunkworks seminars for corporate executives
- How Japan's rising affluence has given the Japanese new confidence; why the era of "catching up" may be over
- The problems labor unions have encountered in trying to organize service-sector workers
- Brazil's return to democracy

Each of these articles contained information about the way the world is changing.

Don't spend so much time on daily newspapers that you skip other reading. Innovators develop shortcuts. To save time, Lewis Lapham, the man who reinvented *Harper's Magazine,* told us he sometimes lets the *New York Times* collect all week before reading it. "What happens is that you see a lot of news is repetitive," he explained. "A lot of what is on page one

79

Wednesday is about what's going to happen or what might happen on Thursday. The operative verb is 'predicted,' 'announced would take place,' 'challenged.' So if you work your way back in time, you can skip all of those stories and just read what really happened. It's amazing, the amount of material that gets eliminated."

7. Develop a System to Organize Your Information

Once you start monitoring trends, you may want to clip and save articles of interest. We suggest you keep articles with specific, helpful information; features about significant national and regional trends; reports on topics you want to learn more about; articles about subjects that interest friends and associates. Ask your friends to do the same for you.

You'll also need a system for organizing the clippings. There really isn't a "better" way—only one that works for you. Take advantage of the many tools available at stationery stores: Hi-Liter pens, X-acto knives for clipping articles, Post-it notes.

Rinaldo Brutoco, the pay-television pioneer, goes through thirty magazines each month and tears out articles of interest. To avoid clutter, he discards the magazines and reads the articles when he has time.

Regis McKenna, the Silicon Valley marketing consultant credited with helping a fledgling Apple Computer polish its image, reads between fifty and one hundred magazines, plus assorted newspapers, every week. He clips articles and creates files for information he wants to retain.

Quality Inns president Robert Hazard keeps a small box labeled "Lodging Trends" on his desk. From his reading, he takes down pertinent information on index cards, which he reviews every evening after work. When he comes across an article he senses may be useful, he clips and files it. He and his team of executives constantly fire articles of interest back and forth with accompanying notes: "Hey, Jerry, did you see this? How does it relate to your area?" In this way, they share information on lodging trends specifically, and broader trends generally.

8. Monitor Other Information-Rich Media

Television has changed us fundamentally, and not just because of the way it instantly brings information from all over the world. Television has also taken time away from the all-important activity of going home after work and thinking about what we've done all day, and even from talking about it with others. Instead, it lulls us into a stupor during which hours disappear. Before long, it's time for bed. We've gained nothing of lasting informational value, and we have nothing to show for our time.

Not surprisingly, innovators spend little time watching the tube. When they do, they watch selectively. They are too busy living their own lives to watch television actors pretending to be someone else. Though TV has entertainment value, its *information* value is low. The payoff for an hour-long program, for example, is roughly equal to reading a ten-minute article.

But television does provide trend-watchers with commercials. Commercials have become an important cultural barometer. Still, if you are learning about new trends for the first time through commercials, your informational intake is a bit thin. Commercials amplify and reflect trends; they don't announce them.

For many people on the go, the radio serves as the main medium of information. Here, call-in talk shows can tip you off to what other people are concerned about, and some of them, such as Talkradio's nationwide "Michael Jackson Show," have one interesting guest after another. National Public Radio is a blessing to many commuters for news and features, with its A.M. "Morning Edition" and its P.M. "All Things Considered." Find out if there is a public radio station in your area and tune in.

Audiocassettes are increasingly becoming part of many people's information diet. Recorded "publications" such as the *Hines Report,* a monthly audiocassette service, provide brief updates on events in the business and financial community. Subjects are researched, written, and taped as short, fast-paced reports. *Newstrack,* another such service, scans seventy business periodicals from *Industry Week* to the *Wharton Magazine* and records selected articles for subscribers.

Here are four more quick tips on how to monitor information-rich media:

1. Broaden your informational intake by attending seminars and lectures.
2. To better utilize television, tape good programs that air when you aren't home. When you're in the mood for TV, watch these instead of whatever happens to be on. By taping the evening news for later playback, you can "zap out" the ten minutes of commercials and get the news in twenty minutes.
3. While driving to and from work, try listening to a different station every day for a week: rock, all-news, all-talk, country, black, Hispanic, Christian, and so on. What perspectives do you pick up? What type of person does each program address? Who advertises on that station and why?
4. Keep a list of books you want to read. Cull new titles from newspapers, magazines, and from asking others what they've read that influenced their thinking. When you go into libraries and bookstores, you'll know exactly what you're looking for.

9. Find Opportunities in the Wave

The ultimate goal of becoming your own trend-watcher is to discover opportunities for yourself. As you begin actively observing change, you'll become adept at distinguishing fads from trends. The media mixes the two (i.e., "fashion trend"), and in fact, "vogue or current style" is a legitimate use of the word *trend.* For our purposes, we use the word *fad* to connote such short-lived phenomena as Hula-Hoops, pet rocks, miniskirts, and Trivial Pursuit. By *trend* we mean those larger forces that set the course of our lives. In *Megatrends,* John Naisbitt wrote about ten new directions transforming our lives. Included were such things as the shift from an industrial society to an information society, the rise of the "multiple-option society" (greater choices in everything we do), the change from centralization to decentralization, and so forth.

There are no hard-and-fast formulas to separate fads from trends, but some things are easier to categorize than others. Certain forces appear inexorable, such as the rising complexity and desire for speed, convenience, and greater choice. Others are matters of fact: The "graying of America," for example, is arising due to the large Baby Boom population making its way through the life cycle, followed by what has been described as a "baby bust." Today's Baby Boom mothers are having fewer children than their parents did and having them later in life. By separating those things which are part of the Wave from those which aren't, we begin to see patterns, and in seeing patterns we can begin to spot problems to solve and opportunities to create.

To take an obvious example, it's easy to recognize that the tobacco industry has a dim future, just as it's obvious the computer industry has a bright one. Even though tobacco is a $19 billion industry, it isn't one that looks promising for someone starting out in a career.

By contrast, consider the fitness trend, which Jacki Sorensen of Aerobic Dancing exploited. Do you think it is short-lived or here to stay? Chances are, it's here to stay. As the nature of the work most of us do (more sedentary, less manual) combines with increasing scientific understanding of how lack of exercise and poor diet contribute to disease and shortened life spans, more people are becoming involved in fitness programs.

Sorensen's experiences illustrate another point: In most instances, innovators don't create the Wave. They merely amplify it and help popularize certain products, services, and methods based on it. Look at the many opportunities created by the fitness trend: health food stores, vitamin manufacturers, "fat farms," exercise equipment manufacturers, aerobic workout studios, health conference centers, health magazines, exercise magazines and books—the list is a long one.

Alexander Graham Bell didn't create the human desire to communicate. Bell rode the Wave by inventing a technology that allowed people to communicate in a new way. Thomas Edison didn't create the desire for a safer way to light homes. He understood where the Wave was headed. He saw that as people moved to the cities they no longer went to bed when the sun set. As a result, they needed a safer way to light their houses than gas provided. That's why Edison worked so hard to perfect the incandescent bulb. But had he stopped there, he would have been just another inventor. There were others who, independently, were avidly developing their own versions of an incandescent bulb. What made Edison an outstanding innovator was that after he invented the bulb, he also created a way for it to be *used* in developing the system for electricity to be delivered to homes and buildings.

Steve Jobs and Steve Wozniak, co-founders of Apple Computer, didn't create the desire to manipulate data electronically and "process" words more efficiently. They merely provided people with a way to perform these tasks easily with a computer that was "user friendly" and less expensive. They rode the Wave when they envisioned that the PC would be useful to larger and larger numbers of people. But they went much further. They turned that vision into a concrete reality called Apple II.

This passionate desire to connect with a customer group drives innovators to exemplify our ninth suggestion on trend-watching. Follow their example by thinking constantly about finding unsolved problems and unfilled needs.

The Wave we speak of is real, its manifestations many. The methods we discussed for observing the Wave can work for you. And the ninth lesson to be learned from innovators is not just to watch, but to watch with an eye toward cashing in on unexploited opportunities.

Why Trend-Spotting Leads to Success

If you haven't kept abreast of the larger forces shaping our world, you may think becoming a trend-spotter will require you to give up your leisure time in the pursuit of information. Effective trend-spotting doesn't have to be time-consuming, but it does require you to alter a few patterns and adjust your mind-set. If Dan Rather is your sole source of news, you need to take action now or face joining the rest of the also-rans.

Professor Herb Dordick of the University of Southern California Annenberg School of Communications divides people into those who are "being informed" and those who are "getting informed." Only 10 percent of the population, he suggests, actively pursues new information. These are the people who are "getting informed." Those who are "being informed" are the ones inundated with information who have no strategy to separate the noise and clutter from that which is useful, valuable, and which fuels their innovation machine.

Will following these nine steps actually turn you into a trend-spotter? Will they really enhance your vision? We believe they will, because we've seen them work for America's leading innovators. Vision is something we can all develop and use. Fred Smith put it this way:

> Vision is just a lot of grinding-it-out information gathering and being willing to make certain assumptions based on the changes that are happening. And sometimes those changes are coming in very different areas and you synthesize them to come up with an idea.

Smith knows whereof he speaks. He discovered a fantastic opportunity by studying the Wave. So can you. Start watching trends and it won't be long before you spot an opportunity others haven't seen yet, one that is ripe for you to exploit.

Provided, that is, you don't let your prejudices block you from acting on it. In the next chapter, we'll show you how to avoid this roadblock by sharing another Secret Skill of innovators: how to unhook your prejudices and keep them unhooked.

FIVE

Unhooking Your Prejudices

**A person with a new idea is a crank
until the idea succeeds.**

Mark Twain

T alk to innovators and one line comes up again and again:
"Everyone told me I was crazy . . . but I went ahead and did it
anyway."

Everyone told Bill Gore he was crazy to leave his secure,
well-paying job as a Dupont research chemist to start a company in his basement. But Gore left anyway. Today W. L.

Gore and Associates manufactures everything from Gore-Tex, the "breathable" yet waterproof fabric, to artificial heart valves and vascular joints. Annual revenues: $190 million.

Everyone told Fred Smith he was crazy to start an overnight package express. "There's no market for such a service," they said. "The Civil Aeronautics Board will never approve it. You won't be able to find reliable couriers. Besides, if there were a market for such a service, the major airlines would already be offering it." Needless to say, Smith "did it anyway."

Everyone told Stuart Karl he was crazy to start an instructional video company. "People are looking to be entertained when they watch television," they said. "You'll spend time building a market and the major publishers will come along and swamp you." They laughed heartily when Karl announced he was trying to interest Jane Fonda in a workout video. "You!" one attorney friend chortled. "Stuart, you've got to be nuts."

The message is clear: If someone hasn't told you lately that your ideas are crazy, you haven't been doing much thinking in the Innovator Mode.

The Problem With Prejudice

Innovative ideas don't come from playing it safe. They don't come from looking at what you are already doing or from trying to do things the same old way. Innovative ideas—those which solve problems and create opportunities—come from fresh, creative trial-and-error thinking. They require us to challenge our assumptions, think outside previous boundaries, and take constant risks. In short, they require that we "unhook" our prejudices.

A prejudice is a judgment or opinion reached before the facts are known or maintained after the facts have changed.

Ridding our thinking of prejudices is critical today. The reason: They limit our ability to respond effectively to change. Here's why:

Prejudice limits vision. It keeps us focused on what already exists, rather than what might exist.

Prejudice stifles creativity. Prejudice insists that there is only one "correct" way of looking at a problem, when in fact there are unlimited ways.

Prejudice prevents problem-spotting. Often the problems innovators solve aren't even clearly identified as such at the time—they're just "the way things are." Before Fred Smith conceptualized Federal Express, people didn't consciously think the lack of an overnight express service was a national problem. They simply thought, *I'm in trouble. This package is supposed to be on Smithers' desk in Denver tomorrow. I sure wish there were some way of getting it there tomorrow.*

Prejudice restricts the inflow of information. The prejudiced person chooses to believe he or she has all the relevant facts rather than choosing to seek out the truth.

A Checkup From the Neck Up*

Tom Wolfe once observed that what a good journalist needs most is a "portable ignorance," the ability to put aside what he thinks he knows in order to receive other points of view without prejudice. Developing a "portable ignorance" lies at the heart of becoming an innovative thinker.

Left to their own devices, our minds tend to look at the world in familiar ways. We stick with assumptions for long periods without determining whether they have any factual foundation. We lose our curiosity, our sense of wonder. People

* Thanks to our good friend Zig Ziglar for this aphorism.

who have become prejudiced no longer pay attention to the environment. They don't look for new patterns; they don't notice anomalies. They stop asking why. Opportunities rush by without them.

Ridding the mind of prejudices does not come naturally. In fact, the older we get the harder it often becomes.

> *You cannot harbor prejudices and innovate at the same time. Innovators realize they gain a strategic advantage by striving constantly for an open, receptive mind. They are tough on themselves in their efforts to avoid prejudice.*

Identifying prejudices must be an ongoing process. We don't unhook and remain prejudice-free for the rest of our lives. Unhooking involves a constant battle against complacency. It involves challenging our assumptions, constantly taking in new ideas, monitoring and guiding our thinking toward the positive, and seeking continuous feedback. In effect, it involves observing how our minds work.

The following checkup is designed to help you inspect your "thinking department." If you think about your typical reaction or response to the 12 statements that follow (rather than the one you know is "correct"), this inventory will give you a rough idea of your predisposition to prejudice. Write out your responses in your idea notebook or on a separate sheet of paper.

1. I would rather know the truth than be right.
2. I often seek no-holds-barred feedback from my spouse, colleagues, friends, and others.
3. I'm often accused of asking too many questions.
4. I believe the opinions of others are helpful most of the time.
5. I like routines and stick by them.

6. I don't believe in seeking counseling unless I've got a serious problem.
7. I make it a point to try to see things from the other person's point of view.
8. I work on trying to look at things with a totally open mind.
9. People find it easy to share their failures and their vulnerable spots with me.
10. I listen unconditionally.
11. I tend to make up my mind quickly with only a little information.
12. I am objective.

What do your responses to these statements reveal?

While everyone is closed to other points of view at times, your success as an innovator depends on the degree to which you can think with a fresh mind. And only you can take steps to "freshen" your thinking.

If you are a manager or an executive, your subordinates probably recognized your prejudices long ago. They may not come out and tell you your thinking is prejudiced. But their opinions may be holding back your team's output. In the Innovation Age, where current, unbiased information and feedback are strategic resources, your employees may be screening the information you receive to cater to your biases. If you are self-employed, your closed-mindedness may go unnoticed by others. After all, nobody really knows how you think, solve problems, or create opportunities for yourself. They see only the results (or lack of them).

How to Improve the Quality of Your Thinking

The more you demonstrate by your actions that you are someone who wants and expects the truth, the more you'll receive. The more you demonstrate that you won't punish those speaking the truth, the more you'll receive. The more truth you choose to let in, the better you'll be at winning the Innovation Game.

Let's look at six ways to improve the quality of your thinking:

1. Constantly challenge your assumptions. In a recent series of full-page ads, TRW, the giant aerospace and data services company, reprinted some of the most prejudiced comments of all time.

Charles Duell, director of the U.S. Patent Office, in 1899: "Everything that can be invented has been invented."

Grover Cleveland in 1905: "Sensible and responsible women do not want to vote."

Robert Millikan, Nobel prizewinner in physics, in 1923: "There is no likelihood man can ever tap the power of the atom."

Lord Kelvin, president of the Royal Society, in 1895: "Heavier-than-air flying machines are impossible."

Today we smile at the shortsightedness of these established experts. In reality, we all make equally faulty assumptions. About ourselves and our potential. About "what the market wants." About our ability to implement our ideas, and thereby to create our futures.

In chapter 3, you were asked to write about any beliefs you felt might be holding you back. We suggested such possibilities as "I don't have what it takes," "I don't have the necessary experience," "I don't have the talent to do what I really want to do," and so forth.

Unless challenged, such assumptions can hold you back. Consider the assumption "I don't have the talent." Is a perceived lack of talent stopping you from doing what you'd like to do? If you answer yes, consider the five-year University of

Chicago study of leading artists, athletes, and scholars. Conducted by Dr. Benjamin Bloom, the research was based on anonymous interviews with the top twenty performers in various fields. These people included concert pianists, Olympic swimmers, tennis players, sculptors, mathematicians, and neurologists. Bloom and his team of researchers from the University of Chicago probed for clues as to how these achievers developed. For a more complete picture, they interviewed their families and teachers.

The report stated conclusively that drive and determination, not great natural talent, led to the extraordinary success of these individuals. Bloom noted, "We expected to find tales of great natural gifts. We didn't find that at all. Their mothers often said it was another child who had the greater talents."

What they found were extraordinary accounts of hard work and dedication: the pianist who practiced several hours a day for seventeen years; the swimmer who rolled out of bed every morning at half-past five to do laps for two hours before school.

What assumptions are you making right now that are holding you back? Are you challenging those assumptions?

The *desire* to challenge assumptions is one reason innovators have such voracious appetites for new information and experiences. Aldous Huxley once said that "experience is not what happens to you but what you make of what happens to you." Innovators realize this instinctively. It is why they soak up all kinds of information wherever they go. They develop a wide range of interests: the developmental stages of infants, how to sell ideas, the various foods of Indian cuisine, Greek philosophy, genetic engineering, the voting records of various congressmen. They keep adding fresh information to their mental files to avoid erroneous or obsolete assumptions.

2. Avoid thinking ruts. Have you ever wondered why so many of today's leading innovators are young men and women in their teens, twenties, and thirties?

For one thing, young innovators aren't betting their reputations. They have little to lose and everything to gain if their ideas prove successful.

But there's another reason youthful innovators are winning big today: the quality of their thinking. Not beholden to any particular way of seeing the world, they are free to do their own thinking, to conceptualize without blinders. Told they have a "crazy idea," they counter with an "I'll show you" persistence that drives them on through the darkest of days.

It's not their youth that is critically important; after all, Ray Kroc was in his fifties when he started McDonald's. Innovators don't allow their thinking to become mired in ruts.

The Rut of Conventional Wisdom. This is merely the consensus of opinion until somebody replaces it with something better. At one time the prevailing paradigm was that the earth was flat. Then someone came along and said the earth was round. The people who had invested heavily in the conventional wisdom stood to lose face with this new theory, so they tried to discredit it.

It's hard to ferret out today's conventional wisdom and where it is wrong. Take the auto industry. Here, a general estrangement between labor and management was viewed for years as a natural state of affairs. The underlying assumption on the part of management was that American blue-collar workers were lazy, irresponsible, contentious, and couldn't be motivated. Organized labor, for its part, viewed management as uncaring, greedy, and intransigent.

Then came the Japanese automobile onslaught of the 1970s. By 1980, one car in five was foreign. Topping that off, in the early 1980s Japanese companies began building factories on American soil.

But the Japanese didn't buy the prevailing conventional wisdom. They didn't share American management's prejudiced view of American workers. And their plants nurtured a noticeably different climate. At the Nissan plant in Smyrna, Tennessee, workers were introduced to quality circles to improve productivity and safety. Their title was "manufacturing technician," not auto worker.

Because they didn't accept the prevailing conventional wisdom, Japanese companies operating in the United States performed better than American corporations, according to a 1985 study by Columbia University's business school. Based on surveys of 159 such companies, the report noted: "The Japanese companies generally outperformed their American counterparts in terms of quality products, the absenteeism rate, the relationship with workers, and their relationship with customers."

At a time when American companies were moving manufacturing operations overseas, the report was particularly embarrassing. The Japanese were beating us at our own game, on our own turf. But to their credit, American automobile manufacturers woke up. First they admitted that conventional wisdom was obsolete in the new era and that labor-management relations would have to be improved. General Motors emulated the Japanese model by designing their new Saturn car manufacturing plant around the theme of worker participation and involvement. Ford made quality "job one." Chrysler, with Lee Iacocca's leadership, reinvented itself from the ground up.

The Rut of Groupthink. Samuel Morse, inventor of the telegraph, was a portrait painter. Robert Fulton, inventor of the steamboat, was a schoolteacher. Before he joined Jack Goeken in building MCI, Bill McGowan owned a small company that manufactured testing devices.

Why is it that innovators are often outsiders? Bill McGowan once answered this way:

> Everyone said we were crazy, but I didn't come from the telephone industry so I didn't have any preconceived notions. What seemed impossible to them did not seem strange to me. We looked over the papers in the Federal Communications Commission library, and we couldn't find anything that said AT&T had the right to a monopoly in telephone service.

Because he was an outsider, McGowan didn't suffer from *groupthink*. Groupthink is evident in all professions, boardrooms, organizations, industries, and societies. Some groups and professions have a stronger tendency to groupthink than others. MIT economist David Birch, founder and chairman of Cognetics, Inc., told us he discriminates against three groups when hiring: economists, MBAs, and engineers. His reasoning:

> They have stereotypical ideas of what their role is and how they should perform their function. They tend to be very cliquish and peer-group oriented and not very creative. I would rather hire a geographer or historian, preferably a liberal-arts person. [At Cognetics] we have almost no technicians, even though we are deeply immersed in computer software. I would rather take a bright, creative person and have him do what we do than somebody who thinks he knows what we do . . . but really doesn't.

To innovate, you can be any age chronologically, but your thinking must be young. By avoiding thinking ruts, the innovator is able to see improvements that others miss. And he is able to see the opportunities where others see only problems.

3. Search for ways to improve your thinking skills. Edward DeBono, physician and founder of the Center for the Study of Thinking at Cambridge University, is an internationally known thinking consultant. In an era of accelerating change, increasing complexity, and heightened competition, interest in the thinking process has increased. DeBono is a pioneer. He has taught thousands of Fortune 500 executives how to improve thinking skills. Public school teachers in Venezuela are required to teach his methods as part of a nationwide self-improvement effort. DeBono's thesis is a simple one: He believes the ability to think *well* can be taught and that thinking ability has very little relationship to a person's intelligence quotient.

"Highly intelligent people often turn out to be poor thinkers for reasons we call the 'intelligence trap,' " DeBono noted. "A highly intelligent person may be able to convince others so well that his position is best that he stifles desire to explore other alternatives. On the other hand, a person less capable of defending his point of view might end up doing more exploring."

Asked whether people with less intelligence can be equally good thinkers, DeBono replied:

> Above a certain level, the operational skills of thinking can be acquired by anyone. The mind is rather like the horsepower of a car, and thinking is like the driving skill. You may have a powerful car but drive it badly. Or you may have a more humble car and drive it well. And of course you can also have a powerful car and drive it well.

To DeBono, explorative thinking is the essence of good thinking. His best-known technique is "lateral thinking," a way of consciously lifting your mind out of its perceptual ruts and trying out new possibilities. Lateral thinking is nothing new. In fact we have all experienced it at one time or another. We describe it as "getting a different perspective" or "standing back and looking at things from a distance."

"Perception works by allowing experience to create patterns which then organize future experience," DeBono says. "Too often we are satisfied with perceptions which make poor use of available experience."

DeBono is right—and America's innovators often instinctively use lateral thinking to jar their perceptions and get the creative juices flowing. For example, Dr. Robert Schuller calls his "possibility thinking." He stumbled upon it out of necessity in 1955, when he was a young minister facing a difficult challenge. Having accepted an invitation to start a new church in rapidly growing Orange County, California, Schuller was advised that it was virtually impossible to find an empty hall that might serve as a temporary meeting place. With only $500, Schuller and family set out for California. In a cafe in Albuquerque, Schuller picked up a napkin and wrote the numbers 1 through 10. He let his imagination run toward all possible meeting places. His list of ten possibilities included "rent a drive-in theater" buried in the ninth position.

"That list," says Schuller, "was my first rudimentary effort in playing a game I would play many times in the next thirty years." As most of the millions who have read his books or seen his weekly "Hour of Power" television program know, it was item 9 on his list that became his first church. "A drive-in theater? You must be crazy!" they said. But the Orange Drive-in Theater became the first meeting place for the Garden Grove Community Church, and possibility thinking has continued to help Robert Schuller. He credits faith in God and possibility thinking for his belief that the now-famous Crystal Cathedral could be built.

4. Develop side interests and hobbies. Lateral thinking, possibility thinking, and other forms of explorative problem solving are all great—as far as they go. They are ways of "priming the pump," of nudging our minds into the Innovator Mode. But creative breakthroughs are often made while our minds are "off duty."

To keep your thinking fresh, free of prejudices, and in top condition, develop hobbies and interests outside your field. For example, Peter Drucker enjoys hiking the Rockies. Ted Turner enjoys sailing. The advantages of other interests are many. In developing interests outside your specialty, you round off your rough edges. And while you are engaged in these outside activities, your conscious mind is kept off your work-related problems, allowing your unconscious mind to sort things out and generate additional ideas.

5. Seek constant feedback. Eight times a year, Aerobic Dancing pioneer Jacki Sorensen creates, choreographs, and videotapes a new routine for her twenty-five thousand instructors around the United States. Each new routine is equivalent to a stage show and requires research into music archives and continuing study in exercise physiology. Performing under tight deadline pressure, each new dance workout leaves her exhausted. Nevertheless, Sorensen strives to make the next routine even better than the last. One way she does this is by reading her "rap sheets," suggestions each instructor sends of each new routine.

To live as an innovator, you need ongoing feedback on your "performance." The faster you move through life, the more you need feedback from employees, teammates, and family members.

Innovators are customer-group oriented. They constantly poll their customers to determine how their products and services can be improved. Like Sorensen with her rap sheets, Washington restaurateur Robert Giaimo gives ballots to customers during the American Cafe's periodic menu changes. Giaimo wants to know how customers feel about new menu items, and if one doesn't go over, he changes it.

Giaimo seeks feedback constantly from his network as well:

> If I have a new idea, I go to people and say, "What do you think of it?" I always get better ideas that way. I don't know what genius is and I don't think I'm a genius. Whatever ideas I have, whenever I try them out on people, even if the ideas were right, they can always be improved. So to me success is listening to people and improving one's ability to understand and interpret what they're saying.

Innovative entrepreneurs like Giaimo don't shut themselves off from customers and rely on written reports. It's no coincidence that executives in the volatile high-tech industries were among the first to reject the trappings of power. They realized that trappings can easily become traps. As a result, management innovators like Dr. Andrew S. Grove, president of Intel Corporation, the Silicon Valley chipmaker, and author of *High Output Management,* take great pains to keep in touch with employees, customers, and competitors.

How do you encourage feedback? Ask for it! "Seek out people who don't hold you in awe, who are willing to challenge you, even if they're wrong," advises Richard P. Feynman, the Nobel prizewinning physicist. Unless you encourage them to do otherwise, *most people will tell you what they think you want to hear.* Not only must you encourage honest communication but you must also *continue* to seek it out: "You know, Bill, this is valuable feedback. I really appreciate your taking the time. You may be keeping me from making a big mistake and I'd like to hear your comments on other parts of my idea, too."

By the way you accept feedback, you demonstrate that you appreciate constructive comments. The way you react determines whether you'll receive honest feedback in the future. To ensure that the feedback is unrestrained, you must listen unconditionally. Refuse to allow yourself to become defensive. If someone is critiquing a speech you just gave, for example, *don't try to justify what you said.* Don't explain what you were trying to do. Instead, focus on the person giving the feedback. Use sentences such as, "So what you're saying is that I need to use more vocal variety rather than lapse into a monotone." Nod and react visibly in order to show the person that you are taking it all in. And if you feel yourself wanting to defend your performance, remind yourself that the person talking to you has prejudices too. Hence, listen to what he has to say and evaluate it later.

As important as feedback is, there are times when it can help you clarify your thinking, and times when you must do this for yourself. In thinking through an idea, to whom you go for advice is important. Try to choose people who will be honest. If you share your idea with someone in the Sustainer Mode, he or she may dampen your enthusiasm. Although it is crucial to analyze ideas with others, it is just as important who those persons are, how many risks *they* have taken, and how objective and knowledgeable they are. Seeking out the right persons to give you feedback, especially on a Breakthrough Idea, is a feat in itself, which we'll have more to say about in chapter 9.

6. Avoid thinking of yourself as an expert. In discussing her own training as a teacher, Marva Collins said:

> I didn't know anything about educational theory, and I have often thought that worked in my favor. Without pre-

conceived ideas and not bound by rules, I was forced to deal with my students as individuals, to talk to them, listen to them, find out their needs. I wasn't trying to see how they fit into any learning patterns or educational models. I followed my instincts and taught according to what felt right. I brought my own experiences into the classroom, trying to figure out how I had learned as a student. I remembered what had bored me and what had interested me, which teachers I had liked and which ones I had disliked, and applied it all to my teaching. Not having any formal theory or textbook methodology to follow made me *receptive to new ideas*. I was *constantly learning* along with my students, always looking for new ways to make a lesson more exciting. [Italics added.]

Sir Clive Sinclair, the British inventor of the pocket calculator and the flat-screen television, among other things, has said that when he enters a new field, he reads "just enough to get a base, just enough to get the idiom" of the field but doesn't do an exhaustive survey.

Innovators are often youthful and often newcomers to a field. Yet can being an expert actually prevent the hatching of innovative ideas? Henry Ford thought so. He once described an expert as a man who "knew all the reasons an idea wouldn't work."

But is ignorance really the key to innovation? Hardly. Marva Collins learned how to teach by sheer determination of will and openness to what worked. Sinclair is one of the most knowledgeable inventors of our time. To live as an innovator you do need knowledge of your field—the more the better. Otherwise you might spend a year working on a brilliant idea—only to find out it has already been tried and found wanting.

So to be an innovative thinker you need to do two seemingly contradictory things:

1. Develop all the expertise you can, but
2. Avoid thinking like an expert.

Both are critical to the success of innovators.

Develop expertise. Observe the thinking of innovators and leaders in your field. How do they think about problems? How do they keep abreast and monitor trends? Which trends do they consider most influential? And most important, how do they solve problems and create opportunities?

You can identify these leaders by reading trade publications and by talking to others in your field. When reading, ask yourself what names keep reappearing. Who is quoted most often? Who is being profiled by the media?

Once you identify these individuals, read what they have written and what has been written about them. Seek them out in the flesh: Attend their lectures and seminars. Make personal contact. You might even start a file on each of them. Ask yourself questions constantly: What are they doing differently that sets them apart, makes them unique? What information sources do they tap that I might tap? What is there about their product or service or personal style that I can adopt and use?

What you are likely to find by studying these pioneers is that, on the surface, they don't appear to be operating that much differently. But look closer. What sets them apart is that they are more focused on the future, more determined, more tuned in to the places where ideas happen. They pick up many of their ideas the same way they absorb information: by being alert and open. When some new information or idea comes along, they pay attention. They put it in their mental files or write it down to ponder later.

Avoid thinking like an expert. While there are dangers in trying to innovate without knowing your field thoroughly, there are, likewise, dangers in thinking of yourself as an expert,

103

especially an *acknowledged expert*. The biggest danger is that of losing your sense of wonder. Instead of being driven by curiosity, you become driven to defend that which you have previously researched, invented, created, marketed, recorded. You begin reciting "safe" and "proven" answers; you stop uttering those three simple words, "I don't know."

What then? For a while, nothing. Your colleagues still see you as the expert. Reporters still call you for your comments. Audiences still applaud your speeches. But the seeds of your downfall have been sown. The world keeps on turning and before long, someone less prejudiced will eclipse you. He will improve on your invention; deliver the same service for less; add value to "your" product; conduct research that makes yours obsolete. When this happens, you're out of the game. Unless, that is, you can unhook your prejudices and get back in the Innovator Mode.

Innovators who continue to innovate throughout their lives never forget that there is always more to learn. Although they may be teachers by virtue of their knowledge and experience, they continue to think of themselves as students.

A Final Point About Prejudice

Try as we might, we can never entirely rid our thinking of prejudice. The best we can hope for is to continuously exchange one set of prejudices for another superior set. This point was eloquently brought home in a conversation with California industrial psychologist Donald Moine, who has helped hundreds of sales professionals improve their performance:

I don't believe in the concept of ultimate truth. I believe very much that the sensory system is extremely limited.

104

There's a hawk out that window who can see things that you and I can't even see. There's a dog here who can hear things we can't even recognize as sound. Even on a sensory level we take in a fraction of the amount of information that's available. There is incredible mental distortion based upon our past programming. Whatever little bit of information is left gets in and we call that truth and reality. Growth and progress and change and innovation are all a matter of dropping old prejudices, and not deceiving ourselves into thinking that we have the ultimate truth. Believing we have the whole truth and all the answers can lead to the greatest horrors in the world: war, oppression, totalitarianism, hatred, racial prejudice, age prejudice, religious prejudice, sexism. When people think they alone have the answers, they feel justified in doing terrible things to other people.

We agree. Believing you are now or ever will be entirely free of prejudice is a prejudice in itself. Successful innovation occurs only within the context of an open mind.

Why drop your prejudices? Perhaps the most compelling reason of all is that prejudices damage your ability to generate and work with new ideas. In the next chapter, we'll take lessons from the nation's most successful innovators so that you too will be able to brainstorm with the best of them.

SIX

Working With Ideas

**I come up with a hundred ideas.
Out of those I reject ninety-nine.**

Ted Turner

From the space shuttle to the money market fund, from the Egg McMuffin to the credit card, every innovation began as an idea in someone's mind. You may be coming up with more ideas than you realize. Everybody has ideas. So do you.

Innovators have an edge because of the way they *work with* their ideas, developing, rejecting, and using them to solve

106

problems and create opportunities. Consider these two examples, one a failure and one a success:

While reading a small-print catalog one day, Wendy came up with the idea of a flat, pocket-sized magnifying lens similar to the kind recreational vehicles have on their back windows. Wendy was excited about the concept and spoke with an attorney, who encouraged her to pursue it. Next, she called the vice-president at a lens manufacturing company, who asked her to put the idea in writing and submit it.

But somehow Wendy never got around to it, promising herself she'd do it "next week." Finally, she forgot about it. Two years later, in a variety store, Wendy was jolted by the realization that someone had acted on the very same idea.

Amy Clelland was a nine-dollar-an-hour electronics assembler at the Burroughs plant in Mission Viejo, California. Each day she watched as dozens of printed circuit boards were thrown on the trash heap because they contained electrical shorts. It was an expensive waste of time and materials, but conventional wisdom had it that the boards could not be repaired.

With only a layperson's knowledge of electronics, Amy began experimenting. She and her husband drilled holes in the boards and poured in epoxy. Before long she had come up with a solution to the problem. Through the company's employee suggestion plan, Amy submitted her idea, complete with diagrams. The result: Amy was presented with a check for thirty-six thousand dollars. Her idea was implemented in two weeks.

Today, good ideas are welcomed, especially those that save time and money, make life more convenient, or solve problems. The highly competitive, rapidly changing economic climate has intensified demand for new ideas.

Faced with these challenges, many otherwise intelligent,

hardworking individuals falter. They lack confidence in their ability to generate ideas. They procrastinate, pass the buck, or bring in outside consultants.

Tapping Into Your Creativity

How can you improve your "idea quotient"? The first requirement is to think of yourself as an idea person. You are creative! Creativity is already within you; you just need to tap it. Despite the fact that the Innovation Age is upon us, many of us are going around with an age-old prejudice clouding our thinking. This prejudice says, "You either have creativity or you don't."

Gifted is a word that should be struck from the dictionary. It is obsolete. Certainly everyone isn't born with equal talents or abilities. Not everyone is capable of learning to perform brain surgery or paint like Picasso. But anyone can learn to be more creative through the way he or she works with ideas. Creativity, as *Business Week* magazine noted in a 1985 cover story, *can* be learned.

David Campbell, Ph.D., a fellow at the Center for Creative Leadership in Greensboro, North Carolina, and author of *Take the Road to Creativity and Get Off Your Dead End,* has studied creativity for twenty years. He believes there is a myth about creativity that goes like this: "There are those who have it and those who don't." As Campbell explains:

> The people who don't believe they've been blessed with creativity think that it comes far more easily to creative people than it actually does. But if you ask people who use their creativity what the most popular misconception is, they tell you it's that other people think it's easy for them to be creative. The fact is it's not easy. It's really just a lot of hard work. You've got to try and fail, try and fail, and try and fail again.

Campbell's insight is supported by Lee Clow, president and creative director of Chiat/Day Advertising. The firm's distinctive commercials for Apple computers, Nike athletic shoes, and Pizza Hut have garnered a bevy of industry awards. But even for someone who has achieved such recognition, coming up with the next campaign is never easy. Clow told us:

> Mostly, you go down paths that lead nowhere. Sometimes you'll sit in front of a tablet or with three other people in a brainstorming session, and you'll just stare at each other. Absolutely nothing happens. The harder you try to make it come out of your brain, the more suppressed it gets. Then, all of a sudden, bam! What if we did it this way? Or how about that? Many times I've gotten up at four in the morning and gone down to the kitchen and done the story board.

Innovators are creative because they are idea-oriented. They are constantly on the lookout for concepts they can put to use. But they aren't interested in merely conjuring ideas: *They want to move on them.* Once innovators have generated an idea, it is placed on a sort of mental-to-physical-world conveyor belt. It is developed and tested on others; sometimes it's rejected. But if the idea makes it through the process, it is implemented.

How America's Top Marketing Consultant Works With Ideas

Regis McKenna, the Silicon Valley marketing consultant, describes working with ideas this way:

> Most ideas move to other ideas and you build on them. There are many that you don't bring to fruition. You test them, you try them, you bounce them off people. You bring them up in various situations and you discuss them with others. And if you get hit in the head five or six times with a

two-by-four, you say, "Gee, maybe that's not a very good one." There's really no other way to do it. You've got to experiment.

In 1963, when he came to California from his native Pittsburgh, Regis McKenna was a struggling young ad salesman and Silicon Valley was a vast fruit orchard. But today, the burgeoning area south of San Francisco is recognized worldwide as a laboratory of technological innovation and McKenna has become one of the Valley's key players. In addition to helping Steve Jobs and Steve Wozniak develop a winning image for Apple Computer, he has been involved in consulting for companies from 3M to Intel and sits on the board of half a dozen high-tech firms. "Simply being a client of Regis McKenna," *Fortune* once observed, "has become a kind of anointment for a high-tech business."

An avid trend-watcher and idea lover, McKenna was the first to see that his field—marketing and communications— was becoming as sophisticated as his clients' products. Merely sending out press releases to news organizations no longer cut it. Start-up companies, desperately needing "good press," got lost in the slush pile. So McKenna began looking for innovative solutions.

He worked at building trust among the high-tech "infrastructure"—that tight-knit group of financial analysts, luminaries, journalists, and industry-related experts who influence investor confidence in companies. Only *after* he had formed good personal relations with these individuals did he seek media attention for a client company.

In 1975, McKenna was asked to help launch America's first retail computer store. This store, which would spawn the Computerland chain, was, at the time, a high-risk experiment. There was an abundant need for creative ideas. Since such a store had never existed before, what should it be like? How would it attract customers?

McKenna recalled the dilemma when we interviewed him at his firm's Palo Alto headquarters: "From our collective experience and my own experience, it wasn't like a stereo shop, it wasn't like a camera shop. It wasn't like anything else, because buying a computer was a sizable investment. You couldn't ask someone to spend five thousand dollars on a trial. The customer wasn't comfortable with what to do with a computer. If something went wrong, was it his fault or the computer's fault? So there simply weren't any good analogies to go to."

How did McKenna come up with the ideas he needed? How does he sort out the winners from the duds?

"I see creativity and ideas as something you practice," McKenna responded. "When there's an unknown quality, you experiment. There is no prescription for how to succeed in business except that you must experiment and be willing to respond and react quickly. So you move two steps ahead, one step backward. You're constantly experimenting with things that work or don't work. You have to have a sense of the future, of experimenting with the future, coming up with creative solutions nobody has tried before."

Much of McKenna's business day is consumed by meetings. Yet wherever he goes, he takes along his idea notebook and jots down ideas as they occur. "You're sitting there in a meeting and something is said that relates to something else you're thinking about in some other area. And then your mind starts thinking about that. I'm always in this mode of looking for a new idea, or a new or better way of doing something."

McKenna is a big user of idea files. He showed us the contents of a file marked "Second Product Failures." The idea had occurred to him that the second product of many entrepreneurial companies had a tendency to fail, or at least not to meet the success levels of the first product. He wanted to study the problem further. By keeping notes on the idea he hoped to spot a pattern which might reveal the cause of these failures. The file contained his notes, magazine and newspaper clippings, and miscellaneous sales reports and marketing data on a variety of second products. In addition, his research department taps various data bases to locate additional information on topics. All this is supplemented by his own observations. McKenna has found that such effort pays off:

> You build up your knowledge base that way, and you're equipped to take advantage of situations that come along much more quickly. You have to think fundamentally—get down to the essence of an idea in order to deal with it. For example, on why second products fail, I'll go out and interview these people. Did they use the first product as a model for the second? Was the first product the idea of an individual and the second the product of a committee? I'll need to look at what I come up with to know if my suspicions are founded. When you get in the habit of looking for patterns in your conversations with people and in the things you read, you can start gathering them together and build up your knowledge base. I get most of my ideas out of that process.

Ten Proven Strategies for Working With Ideas

As McKenna's example illustrates, working with your ideas requires that you take them seriously. Pay attention when an idea occurs to you. Get into the habit of writing down ideas, evaluating them, and implementing the good ones.

Improving your ability to come up with ideas is something that happens through practice. What follows are ten strategies gleaned from successful innovators:

1. Inspect your idea factory. How often do you come up with imaginative solutions and bring them to fruition?

One way to check yourself is to look at your "things to do" list. That's one collection of your ideas. What does your list reveal about the ideas you work with? Are the items nothing more than daily duties—pick up the dry cleaning, pay the bills, and so on? Everybody must take care of such details, of course. But if these are the only items on your agenda, your idea factory needs retooling. It's not that you aren't generating ideas. The problem is that you aren't *moving on them in systematic fashion.* You are slighting big ideas while spending time on the details. You'll never get ahead this way; at most you'll only catch up.

Try this for a week: Carry a small notebook with you wherever you go and jot down ideas as they occur. Examples might be: "Look into attending computer seminar sponsored by the company." "Discuss with spouse best time to paint house." "Investigate going back to school to earn MBA." "Meet with sales department about starting promotional campaign for the new product line."

The purpose of this exercise is to start you capturing the many ideas that flash into your mind. Later, you can go back and sort through them. Some you'll reject; others you'll want to implement right away. Still others will require further development.

As you develop the habit of capturing your ideas, you'll not only become better at sorting through them but you'll also start coming up with more and better ones. Self-employed people have an advantage here; they can see clearly how an idea develops and where it leads. Conversely, they know that without an idea, nothing gets started.

Whether or not you are self-employed, you will benefit from taking your ideas seriously. Start by inspecting your idea factory's recent output and see what improvements can be made.

2. Look for ideas by studying problems. When we visited Bill

Gore, Chairman of W. L. Gore and Associates and inventor of Gore-Tex, he described his favorite method of generating ideas. "I walk through the plant and I see a piece of equipment that's being built in the shop," Gore said. "I inquire about how it's designed. And I scratch my head and say, 'You know, it would be so much easier, so much better, if it could be done this way instead of that way. Why don't we do it that way?' "

Management by walking around (MBWA) isn't the only way to come up with ideas, but it's a good one. You have to spot problems before you can create ideas to solve them. Perhaps this is why innovators are such active individuals. They prefer to get out and see firsthand. They are constantly asking themselves questions: What problems exist that I can solve if I focus on them? Where are the bottlenecks in this system I've created (or am in charge of)? What do people keep asking for that we don't have?

Identifying the problem, then, is critical. After you've spotted it, solutions must be generated. You can add to your problem-solving abilities by reading about how others do it in their fields. If you are an entrepreneur, read about problem solving in genetic research. If you're an architect, read about problem solving in fashion design or in importing. There are certain logical steps and processes you'll pick up by reading how others solve problems.

Another method is to create an analogy. Analogies are a way of reducing complex problems to manageable proportions. By using analogies ("This transition phase of the business is going to be as challenging to operate as an astronaut operating a rocket pack"), you can extend the common elements of a problem toward a solution. What you are doing is trying to jar your thinking out of the usual grooves and into looking at the problem afresh.

3. Experiment with new ideas constantly. Thomas Edison once suggested that if you wanted to have a good idea, have lots of them. It's true. The willingness to experiment and to fail is the key to working successfully with your ideas.

Wayne Silby, co-founder of the Bethesda, Maryland-based Calvert Group, an investment concern with $2 billion in assets, is highly regarded as a financial services innovator. In 1977, Silby created the first variable rate fund in America. In 1981, he conceived and marketed the Calvert Social Investment Fund, which has over $100 million in assets and has become the industry model.

Coming up with new ideas is the most important thing Silby does. But he is the first to admit that not all of his ideas are winners. "As the chairman of this company," Silby told us, "I make sure people recognize that I come up with ideas; that some of them are good and that most of them are bad. What we have to do together as a management team is to sort out the good ones from the bad ones."

Even with innovators like Silby, most ideas are never acted on: They are rejected or evolve into better, stronger ideas. Bounce your ideas off people whose judgment you trust. Encourage their honest feedback. Don't become so emotionally attached to a new concept that you can't bear to have others help you evaluate it. Be willing to have a dud now and then. Experiment constantly.

4. Go for quantity when generating ideas; strive for quality when evaluating them. When you've got a tough problem to solve or decision to make, try to come up with as many ideas—good, bad, "off the wall," totally serious—as you can. Let yourself go; make lists of possible solutions, alternatives, possibilities. Think! But while you're brainstorming—whether alone or in a group—avoid the temptation to pass judgment on the idea.

Later, after you've allowed yourself some time away, come back to the problem. This is the time to evaluate those ideas which seem strongest, to decide whether or not an approach is doable, and whether you need more information before you can tell. Eliminate those with obvious flaws.

Key: Don't attempt to create ideas and evaluate them at the same time. Studies and the experience of the best innovators show that the effect of trying to do both at the same time undermines the creative process.

5. Enhance your environment for maximum creativity. When and where do you do your best thinking?

If there's a time of day when you feel you do your most creative thinking, try to reserve it for yourself and use it to its fullest. If there's a particular spot that says "idea space" to you—your study or the bathtub—set aside time to use that space, alone and free of noise and distraction. Check out places outside your home, too: a park, a library, even a reasonably quiet coffee shop. Find a place where you feel safe to think and dream creatively.

Consultant and best-selling author Tom Peters finds that ideas start percolating while he's cruising the open highway or when he's in the shower. During a break at one of his Skunk Camp seminars at Pajaro Dunes, he said, "I also find I get ideas by listening to people in places like this. It works best for me to try and translate those ideas quickly into something pragmatic: an article or speech I'm working on, for example."

Wayne Silby, the financial-services innovator, favors floating in his isolation tank to "see what bubbles up." Leland Russell, chairman of Eiger Corporation, finds many of his best ideas come to him when he gets up early and putters around in his study listening to classical music. San Francisco designer

Laurel Burch, chairperson of Laurel Burch, Inc., observes that she gets most of her new ideas when she puts her mind to work "mopping up" the details of previous ideas.

Not long ago, Robert Tucker worked on a major project with Rinaldo Brutoco, the pay-television pioneer and chairman of San Francisco-based Dorason Corporation. For a major creative session, Brutoco flew my wife, Carolyn, and me to Kauai, where we stayed with the Brutocos in a condominium on the bluffs above the Pacific. Since this was to be a short "working vacation," we planned to eat out. But right after we arrived, Brutoco suggested he and I go pick up "a few snacks." At the supermarket, he began filling the cart as if he hadn't eaten in days. Bottles of juices, fresh pineapples and island fruits, exotic cheeses and spreads—the bill came to over two hundred dollars. Driving home, I asked him who all the food was for. "Us!" His reasoning: When you're doing intense creative work, be good to yourself and set it up so you don't have to "take time for lunch," which could cost you your momentum. We began working, ideas began flowing, and the wisdom behind his extravagance became evident. If we'd had to go out for lunch, we might have lost momentum. Instead, drinking juices and snacking occasionally, we were able to turn out a respectable body of work each day and still take the late afternoons off.

Brutoco was consciously enhancing our creative environment. But you don't have to spend two hundred dollars or fly to Kauai to enhance yours. In fact, you can do things to your office to turn it into a better place to brainstorm ideas. Take Leland Russell, for example. Not satisfied with traditional executive office design, Russell created his own, integrating his self-study of ergonomics with the personal work space requirements of an executive whose motto is "Fast is good; faster is even better."

Instead of a desk, Russell installed a customed-designed "work station" in a corner of his rectangular-shaped suite. On top of it sits his personal computer with its disc drive, printer, and plotter neatly tucked away inside. "It's a work station, not a power station," Russell told us. "I don't need a big, imposing desk that takes up half the room to impress people." From here, Russell "conferences" with Eiger's far-flung executives, accesses numerous public and private data bases, and performs tasks which require the use of his personal computer.

The office is noticeably quiet; only the sound of occasional conversations or the soft patter of printers can be heard above softly playing classical music. Support staffers work in comfortable, modernistic cubicles with oak desks and full-length views of the Santa Monica Mountains.

For meetings, guests are seated in plush swivel chairs around a four-by-ten-foot oak conference table. At the far end of the table is a twenty-five-inch video monitor, onto which Russell can beam up from his personal computer whatever information he wants—from a meeting's agenda to color-coded sales figures. And if he wants to illustrate a point by drawing or writing freestyle, there's a built-in three-foot artist's easel located nearby. On the opposite wall is an etagere containing an audio system, slide projector, and videotape machine, all of which have wireless, hand-held remote controls. And finally, for more relaxed one-on-one meetings, Russell added an intimate "conversation area" in one corner of the room, complete with elbow-shaped couch.

Why go to such extremes? Russell explained:

> The purpose of the office design and the "tech tools" it contains is to facilitate creativity and communication. Real estate investment is an information-intensive field, one in which information can easily overload its handlers

in the endless details of processing it and understanding what it means. Or it can be handled routinely so that the machines do the work and people have the clarity left to do the thinking. That's what we have attempted to do.

6. Seek out idea-oriented people. It was amazing how many of the innovators we interviewed told us they got most of their ideas from being around other idea-oriented people. They get "fired up" during their conversations and often come away with dozens of new ideas. Idea people are friends, colleagues, co-workers, and neighbors who use ideas in their own lives. They are people who get excited when you express your ideas, and who enjoy talking about their own.

"I love to talk to people who have suggestions," said Sandy Gooch, founder and chairperson of the Los Angeles-based Mrs. Gooch's Natural Foods Ranch markets. "Not only to our employees and customers, but other people in the industry and people in entirely unrelated fields." Gooch described the "amazing dialogue" she often has with her friend Doug Greene, publisher of the *Natural Foods Merchandizer,* a leading trade magazine for the natural foods industry. Whenever she and Greene meet for a brainstorming session, she fills up pages and pages of a legal pad with notes and ideas she wants to follow up on.

Take a moment right now and make a list of the people you know who stimulate your creativity when you are around them. Then ask yourself how you can arrange to spend more time with these people without slighting your other responsibilities. If there aren't such persons in your life right now, resolve to do something about it. Attend meetings of organizations in your field or profession. Through conscious effort, you can and will increase the number of idea people you count as friends.

7. Draw out the creativity of others at every opportunity. Around idea-oriented people, you'll pick up all kinds of information—but not if you dominate the conversation. Make it a point to draw out creative interests and ideas by asking questions. Everybody has an idea or two to give you if you are respectful enough to get them talking about what *they* do and what *they* know. Draw out the creativity of others at every opportunity. Find out what *they* are interested in. Discover what makes them tick. You'll be surprised how much your own ideas will be influenced by listening to others tell you about theirs.

8. Impose deadlines on yourself. Thomas Edison had an interesting habit. Whenever he hatched an idea, he would call a press conference and announce his latest creation. Then he'd go back to his lab and invent it.

There's nothing like a deadline to start you generating ideas. Commit your deadline to paper. Then tell people who are supportive of your efforts. As Tom Peters says, "Announce your product, announce your service, announce your seminar or your book. Then figure out what you've got to do to make it happen."

Robert Hazard of Quality Inns does much the same thing and jokingly calls it the Cortes Theory of Management. When the explorer Hernando Cortes landed in Mexico in 1519, his men wanted to go back to Spain. Cortes burned his ships and announced that he was marching on Mexico City.

Hazard calls in the business press and announces his five-year plan. He gives specific goals for growth and acquisitions of new franchise hotels. The payoff, he told us, is that "it tells all your people where your goals are. And we all feel compelled to meet those goals."

Deadlines will help you overcome the fear of actually doing

something with your ideas. Action conquers fear. Act once and you won't be so hesitant the next time.

9. Look for ideas you can apply from other fields. The California Council of the American Institute of Architects recently sponsored a conference entitled "Sources of Inspiration." The sources identified included: being "inspired"; needing to meet a payroll; fearing failure; seeing the designs of others in magazines; serving the complex needs of clients and those who eventually will use the structure; enjoying the process of creating the structure; or simply wanting to create. "The reality of my inspiration is that I look at a lot of magazines," one prominent architect told his colleagues.

Not so dramatic, are they? Many sources of inspiration *aren't* very dramatic, or even original. Yet another misconception about innovators and creativity is that their ideas are original. Innovators get ideas like everybody else: They dream up some of them, but they borrow many others and combine them to serve their own purposes.

Washington restaurateur Robert Giaimo borrowed the computer display monitor from the airline industry, because he envisioned how it could enhance communication between cooks and waiters in his American Cafes. He observed that there were large hotels that served various restaurants from a central kitchen, and there were commissaries that cooked certain products to ship out.

Robert Hazard of Quality Inns divides ideas into two categories: "lifters" and "poppers." Those in the former category are borrowed from other industries and lodging chains. The "poppers" come out of his own thinking process. Hazard uses an abundance of both. The chain's no-smoking rooms was a lifter. Market segmentation was a popper.

10. Devise a system for capturing your ideas. Ideas are like butterflies: If you have inspected your idea factory and have followed some of the previous suggestions, you may have noticed how ideas can flutter away from you if you don't have your net ready. As we've already discussed, when you try to pin them down on the mounting surface, many of them fall apart. This is why you must capture plenty of them.

Why not rely on memory? Actually, you can. But if you trust your memory, you are in effect making your brain function as a storage bank for your ideas. This can dampen your idea-generation ability, as the mind is preoccupied with holding onto the ideas it has already hatched.

When you are creatively "on a roll" and the ideas start popping, make notes. The simple act of capturing your ideas in a permanent place frees your mind so you feel secure against losing one of your great notions. Here are some other ways of capturing those elusive "butterflies":

Three-by-Five-Inch Cards. Trend-spotter Graham Mollitor, president of Public Policy Forecasting, Inc., of Potomac, Maryland, never leaves home without a pack of them in his vest pocket. He keeps a few of them next to his bed in case he gets an idea in the middle of the night. "Every single idea I have goes down on three-by-five cards. I like to say I write a book a thought at a time, a sentence, a paragraph, an idea at a time. I can open my files and show you hundreds and hundreds of cards," Mollitor said.

Tape Recorders and Pocket Dictation Machines. Many journalists and authors rely on the cassette tape recorder during idea-generation sessions. They let it capture the good stuff *and* the not-so-good. Then later, they'll either transcribe it themselves (a good way to generate further ideas) or they'll hire a transcriber to type up the comments. The other advantage of the recorder is that you can listen to exactly how the ideas were expressed. If the idea was a concept that you in turn want to communicate to your team or your employees, you've captured the perfect expression of it right there. And, if you're preparing a speech from these notes, you have a record of the well-turned phrases.

You can also capture butterflies by taping speeches and seminars. Here the information is coming at you faster than you can absorb it. If it happens to be a great speech, you've captured it—along with the ideas it contains—for later reference. Driving to work, you can relisten through your tape player.

Many innovators who are on the go a lot prefer pocket dictation machines. They're small enough to fit into your breast pocket or purse and you can download wherever you are.

Idea Notebooks. Many innovators keep an idea notebook to capture ideas, impressions, insights, thoughts, and observations that might later be useful. The insights you capture at the time might seem brilliant. When you return to them later, they look devoid of merit. Other times, you'll write down an idea that still seems good later or that triggers a further insight.

Post-it Notes. Every time an idea enters Leland Russell's mind, he writes it down on a Post-it note (the Breakthrough Idea of 3M innovator Art Fry) and sticks it on the surface of his desk. That way he has "captured the butterfly" and he is free to go on generating other ideas without feeling he must make a mental note to remember the idea.

Organizers. These sectioned notebooks with names like Day-Timer, Filofax, or Day Runner are increasingly popular. Those who use them say it is helpful for them to have various categories to store ideas within. Leland Russell, who travels frequently, uses a ten-terminal schedule notebook called Time Design. Each terminal, or section, of the notebook is devoted to a different aspect of his business or personal life: Terminal

123

one is corporate, terminal two is product, three is market, four is property, five is services, six is agenda ("anything I need to talk to somebody about goes in there"), seven is personal ("it might be an idea about my son's education"), eight is the book he's working on, and terminals nine and ten are flexible and are used for special projects.

Russell doesn't always write in the book when he has an idea, but he says it's a matter of processing the idea in some fashion. Russell uses the front of the notebook, called the "input section," for jotting down ideas he gets while driving or at other times when he's too busy to explore them but wants to capture them.

Decide right now on the "capturing system" that works best for you. If you aren't used to capturing your ideas, you may want to experiment with various methods. But if you are to become a proficient idea person, you must decide on a system and use it.

Virtually every innovator we interviewed had some method for capturing his or her ideas, and they would often be able to put their hands on it without moving from where they happened to be sitting. That says something about the importance they place on their ideas. They realize that in this fast-paced world, good ideas may flutter in and out of our minds and be lost forever in the next distraction. Unless you are able to discipline yourself enough to write down your ideas, your chances of working with them are extremely limited. But apply the strategies outlined above and they can have a profound effect on your success.

Innovators: Doers and not Dreamers

Everyone *has* ideas, but innovators *work* theirs through the various stages of development toward implementation. They constantly use ideas to solve problems and create additional opportunities. This is what makes them *doers* and not *dreamers*. They do not wait for ideas to come along. They constantly pull good ideas out of other people, other fields, and other professions. Because they treat ideas with respect, they are better able to select from their many concepts and strategies those that hold the greatest probability of success.

How do they sort out their "breakthroughs" from their "bombs"? One method they use may surprise you: It's a powerful, little-talked-about success secret known by a single word. That word is *intuition,* and it's the subject of our next chapter.

SEVEN

The Power of Informed Intuition

The really valuable factor is intuition.

Albert Einstein

How often have you had a bad feeling about a business deal or relationship, yet gone ahead anyway?

After the relationship turned sour, you probably recalled the faint alarm that went off in your head—your intuition. Everyone has intuition, but not everyone listens to it. Thus they are unable to use it as an internal navigation system to guide their decisions and point the way to the future. In an ever more fast-paced world, intuition is an indispensable tool. Innovators realize this, and it is one of the major reasons they are able to make smart decisions. To live as an innovator, you must sensitize yourself to your intuition and what it is trying to tell you.

What Intuition Is and Isn't

The industrial society was a highly rational, analytical, "prove it" society. Man learned to build large-scale organizations that relied on evidence, control, and order. To the industrial-age thinker, intuition was a throwback to an earlier, "primitive" era before scientific management replaced "seat of the pants" and "gut feel" management. Intuition was often misunderstood, discounted, and confused with the stuff of fortune-tellers and palm readers.

Unfortunately, it still is today.

Many who think of themselves as highly intuitive are also prone to guessing or gambling. Intuition has nothing to do with guessing. It is not impulsiveness or wishful thinking or laziness. It is not a tendency to be too optimistic or too pessimistic. Nor is it the opposite of rational analysis.

Intuition is that part of our minds that throws us subtle hints, suggestions, and faint signals (and sometimes not so faint). It's a people-reading device; a trend-spotting mechanism; a pattern-recognition system. Webster defines it as "the direct knowing or learning of something without the conscious use of reasoning." Let's stick with a shorthand definition: Intuition is "knowing something without knowing how you know it."

For the purposes of this book, we will focus on "informed intuition," intuitive suggestions that arise from experience and perceptiveness. Perhaps chairman of the Washington, D.C.-

based American Cafe chain, Robert Giaimo, described intuition best:

> To me it's accumulated experience in similar situations. You're doing some kind of internal extrapolation. Gut instinct ultimately has an internal logic, but maybe it's not a logic you can document on a piece of paper. It's a lot of internal information and there's something connecting that internal information inside of you that translates into experience. That experience is putting together analysis to a problem.

Intuition's Role in Innovation

Intuition plays an integral role in the way innovators create ideas, make decisions, solve problems, and read people. In conversation, they point to dramatic instances where intuitive flashes have shaped their actions. Businesses are launched on the basis of an intuitive leap. Multimillion-dollar decisions are made on the basis of an intuitive judgment. There is no other way to navigate in a time of accelerating change, increasing complexity, and intensified competition.

Now that the academic community is beginning to unhook its prejudices about the role of intuition, our knowledge of how it functions will likely increase in coming years. Today, we are just beginning to develop the language to describe its function. Nevertheless, there seems little doubt about its important role in winning the Innovation Game. Researcher Weston Agor tested the intuitive abilities of more than two thousand managers at all levels of responsibility in business, government, and other organizations. "Without exception," he concluded, "the top managers in every organization rated significantly higher than middle- and lower-level managers in their ability to use intuition on the job."

To conduct his research, Agor, a corporate consultant and director of the public administration program at the University of Texas at El Paso, used the Myers-Briggs Type Indicator Test, a thirty-year-old personality test that, among other things, measures intuitive ability. Agor discovered that successful executives use intuition in a variety of ways: to size up people they are dealing with; to make quick decisions such as in negotiating sessions when they must "think on their feet"; and in making decisions when all the facts simply aren't available. Top-level executives, Agor reports, must rely not only on available facts but also on "feel." He reports:

> Any time decisions must be made quickly, or an issue is so complex that complete information is not available, the managers who have developed their intuition will have an advantage over those who have not. In the rapidly changing, complex world of the future, these situations will be more and more common.

Harvard business professor Daniel Isenberg reached similar conclusions. Isenberg studied the thought processes of sixteen senior managers in companies ranging from Fortune 500 corporations to ten-million-dollar entrepreneurial firms. He spent an average of two and a half days with each executive. He observed them as they worked, interviewed them about decision making, and led them through exercises designed to capture their thoughts as they went about their work.

"High-level decision makers seldom if ever think in terms simplistically thought of as 'rational,' " Isenberg wrote in the *Harvard Business Review.* "On the contrary, they frequently bypass the rational process altogether, particularly when faced with highly complex problems or issues for which there are no precedents. While decisions are often justified by data and logic, and executive decision making is made to appear 'rational' . . . being 'rational' does not best describe what the manager presiding over the decision-making process thinks about or *how* he or she thinks."

Isenberg found that the senior managers use intuition in at least five different ways:

1. To help them sense when a problem exists.
2. To rapidly perform well-learned behavior patterns.
3. To synthesize isolated bits of data and experience into an integrated picture.
4. To check on the results of rational analysis. (They search until they find a match between their "gut" and their "head.")
5. To bypass in-depth analysis to come up with a quick solution.

What Intuitive People Have in Common

It shouldn't be surprising that today's movers and shakers rely on their intuition. They always have.

Carl Jung, who with Sigmund Freud founded modern psychoanalysis, was among the first to describe the intuitive personality. Jung viewed intuition as one of the four psychological functions; the others are sensation, thinking, and feeling. His description of the "extraverted intuitive" fits many of today's leading innovators:

> The intuitive is never to be found in the world of accepted reality-values, but has a keen nose for anything new and in the making. Because he is always seeking out new possibilities, stable conditions suffocate him. He seizes on new objects or situations with great intensity, sometimes with extraordinary enthusiasm, only to abandon them cold-bloodedly, without any compunction and apparently without remembering them, as soon as their range is known and no further developments can be divined.

130

Jung acknowledged that the extraverted intuitive is "uncommonly important both economically and culturally" and he observed that many tycoons, entrepreneurs, and speculators were among this group. Jung saw the potential for great social good coming from people with this particular personality, and also the extremely high chance that they might self-destruct. (More about this latter tendency in chapter 12.)

"If his intentions are good, i.e., if his attitude is not too egocentric, he can render exceptional service as the initiator or promoter of new enterprises. He brings his vision to life, presents it convincingly, and with dramatic fire, he embodies it. And his capacity to inspire courage or to kindle enthusiasm for anything new is unrivalled, although he may already have dropped it by the morrow."

Since Jung, a number of attempts have been made to measure intuitive ability. Psychologist Malcolm Westcott designed a test to examine how much information people need before they will attempt to solve a problem. Highly intuitive problem solvers, he found, require relatively little information before they are willing to guess at the answer. Westcott's discoveries led him to divide problem solvers into four categories:

1. *Cautious problem solvers.* Require lots of information before attempting to solve problems but are successful in using the information.
2. *Cautious failures.* Require lots of information before attempting to solve problems, and fail to use it successfully.
3. *Wild guessers.* Willing to act on relatively little information, but frequently unsuccessful.
4. *Intuitive problem solvers.* Act successfully on the basis of relatively little information.

Consider what a strategic advantage it is to be an intuitive problem solver. In innovating, you are doing something that

131

has never been done before exactly this way. By definition, all the information is simply not available! When you don't have all the information, you can do one of two things: delay the decision (in which case you stand to lose the opportunity) or rely upon intuition.

What gives certain people the ability to guess accurately when they don't have all the information? Westcott had this explanation:

> They tend to be unconventional and comfortable in their unconventionality. They are confident and self-sufficient, and do not base their identities on membership in social groups. . . . Their investments appear to be primarily in abstract issues . . . [and] they explore uncertainties and entertain doubts far more than the other groups do, and they live with these doubts and uncertainties without fear.

And Westcott had more to say:

> They enjoy taking risks, and are willing to expose themselves to criticism and challenge. . . . They describe themselves as independent, foresighted, confident, and spontaneous.

In short, Westcott's subjects sound a lot like innovators. Innovators, however, don't use the intuitive side of their brains only for problem solving. Let's examine how innovators also use intuition for spotting trends, making decisions, creating ideas, and working with others.

How Intuition Can Help You Spot Trends

If you act on some of the suggestions in chapter 4, you will become adept at trend-watching. But to innovate, you must *spot* trends as well. This requires intuition. The fact is, the many forces and events shaping the future are too complex to be modeled. There is simply no computer program that can predict tomorrow's economy, tomorrow's consumer wants, tomorrow's shortages, tomorrow's technological breakthroughs. Trend forecasters, survey researchers, and futurists are able, at best, to detect trends early and make educated guesses as to how these trends might increase in size or significance.

Because predicting the future is an art rather than a science, the best trend-spotters are those capable of using both sides of the brain. The cautious quantifiers of this genre are lost without an ability to make intuitive connections. One economic forecasting firm makes no bones about its use of a right-brain, intuitive approach in seeking out the future. That company is New York-based Inferential Focus, whose four partners inform their intuition by reading two hundred magazines and trade journals a month, ranging from *Industrial Hygiene News* to *Pipeline and Gas Journal.* By reading this many publications, and thinking about what they are reading, the partners attempt to spot anomalies and make intuitive connections that could portend economic changes. Their insights have proved useful to Fortune 500 corporate leaders, private investors, banks, and even to the White House.

"We're dealing with a world of change, and a crucial element is discovering change," notes Charles J. Hess, one of the firm's partners. The reliance of Inferential Focus on intuition led them, in mid-1985, to conclude that the then "red hot" media sector was due for a fall in stock prices.

This insight may not seem spectacular, but the obscure reasoning points up the type of intuitive connection you can learn to make. Here's how Inferential Focus reached its conclusion: They believed there would be pressure on networks and independent stations to reduce advertising rates. What gave them this idea? The company had its intuitive eye on the rapid pro-

133

liferation of the videocassette recorder. What would be the effect as more and more households used the machine, they wondered. Their answer: More and more people would "zap out" commercials and spend more time watching rented or purchased programming. As a result, advertisers would change the way they spent their dollars, and resist rate increases.

In some ways, becoming a trend-spotter is like following a sport. The more you enjoy it, the more information you absorb. The more information you absorb about it, the better you become at predicting what will happen. The more you observe and take an interest in trends and societal change, the better your intuition will perform when you ask yourself fundamental questions: What does this particular trend mean to my business? What will be the big changes in my industry in the next five years?

Using Intuition With People

Robert Bernstein, chairman of Random House, had what we thought was an apt comment about using intuition with people. "In a business that depends entirely on people and not machinery," Bernstein noted, "only intuition can protect you against the most dangerous individual of all: the articulate incompetent."

Bernstein is right. Moreover, publishing isn't the only business that depends largely on people. In an increasing number of businesses, people are the real assets. Thus the growing need to recruit capable employees. Even a self-employed innovator must build relationships with competent, dedicated, honest people. This means constantly making snap judgments about whom to deal with and whom to avoid. Because we must often make decisions based on incomplete information, our intuitive sense about people is our most reliable guide.

Chicago master teacher Marva Collins relies on her intuition to help her spot the subtle gestures and looks of students that tell her what a child needs:

> Sometimes when a child comes in and I sense they're depressed, I'll write them a note while I'm still teaching and say, "Can I help?" Usually there's been a problem at home. If a child cries without provocation, I can spot that it's not me, that something else is wrong. This year we had a child with a learning disability in our summer school. The first day she couldn't read the test. So she marked everything on the test and then burst into tears. The teachers were trying to make it okay for her. I took her out and told her to forget the test and just learn to read. I think what people assume too many times is that a child is crying just to be crying. But there is another underlying reason there: a problem at home, say. I think you intuitively have to feel these things.

How can you sharpen your intuitive guidance system? First, be honest with yourself. Look back over your life. How would you rate your "people judgment"? Have your relationships generally been good? Or have they brought you pain and suffering? When we're needy, whether it's needing to be loved, needing to consummate a business deal, or needing to hire an employee in a hurry, we often don't listen to our intuition. We hear the need rather than hearing what's going on in the back of our minds.

This point was brought home in our conversations with Gifford Pinchot III, chairman of Pinchot and Company, a New Haven, Connecticut, management consulting firm. Pinchot began his career as a small businessman in the metal products industry. He eventually sold his company and, after attending Robert Schwartz's School for Entrepreneurs in Tarrytown,

New York, became convinced that entrepreneurship would have to take place within major corporations if they were to compete in the global economy. His ruminations led him to come up with a Breakthrough Idea he calls "intrapreneurship." As Pinchot explained in his book *Intrapreneuring: Why You Don't Have to Leave the Corporation to Become an Entrepreneur,* the intrapreneur is the individual who takes hands-on responsibility for innovating within an existing organization. Pinchot spoke openly about his intuition when he said:

> Every time I've made a bad decision about a person, when I trusted someone who should not have been trusted, I eventually recall how much I knew about that person before I made the decision. I knew perfectly well that person couldn't be trusted and yet greed or something made me believe the opportunity involved was so great that I didn't listen to what my intuition was trying to tell me.

Pinchot admitted that this particular lesson took him many times to learn, but suggests:

> If you feel when you're going into something that there's something wrong, do not close the deal, whatever it may be. What's happening is someone has wrapped around the lower aspect of your nature and sold you something you know is not going to work. One of the things that's gone wrong in American business right now is that we don't give ourselves permission to hear those signals anymore. We don't give ourselves permission to act on them. We wait until there is some "objective" reason for taking action, instead of taking action as soon as we know something is wrong.

Pinchot offered additional insights on how he uses his intuition as a guide in making judgments about people:

136

If I'm sitting with someone and I feel fearful and I have no reason to be afraid, then I assume it has something to do with what they're thinking. Unless I have good reasons to believe otherwise, I assume that my own emotional screen is relatively clear and that what I'm feeling is in fact a manifestation of the interaction I'm having with this person and not some weirdness on my part. It took me a long time to trust what I was perceiving and to listen to what it was telling me about that person. It's a matter of giving yourself permission to trust your feelings. And you can be wrong, I suppose, but you could be much more wrong if you ignore them.

In hiring situations, Pinchot has people whose judgment he trusts interact with the interviewee. "Every once in a while someone will find a way of communicating to you that so much good is going to happen as a result of your hiring them that you begin to ignore problem signals." By having another person there to discuss it with, he's better able to spot when this occurs.

How to Use Your Intuition to Enhance Your Creativity

Tuning in to your intuition can help you understand your own mental processes. Try asking yourself these questions: When does my mind work best? How do I generate my best ideas? Where do I do my best thinking?

If you take time to write out your thoughts on these questions, you will gain further insight into your own ways of thinking. The next step is to try to understand what shuts you down creatively. Leland Russell, the real estate innovator whose emphasis on creativity extends from his musical taste to the design of his office, admits that certain things "shut him down":

137

Once I learned what those things were, I started avoiding them. Anything that drains your energy or shuts you down, you've got to manage yourself. What you have to do is mentally move up above yourself and observe yourself reacting and saying, "Okay, I'm cruising along, this is great, I'm feeling the flow, everything is great." Then suddenly, I've freaked out, I've shut down, I can't think, I can't work. What is precipitating this? What thoughts am I having that are shutting my systems down? What person did I interact with who shut my systems down? You have to figure out what's charging your batteries, what's giving you that push, and what's creating the pull or the drag. And start identifying how you're reacting because basically all you have to work with is yourself.

Russell's method of mental management can help all of us maintain the Innovator Mode of thinking, because it is attuned to the changes in our society. Here's how Russell describes it:

What I'm really seeing is that more and more of us are beginning to deal in a conceptual world, a world of abstractions. We're not doing physical things. Even the way we go about implementing an idea is mental. How am I going to make this idea happen? How am I going to get the capital? How am I going to get the people enrolled? We're dealing with a society in transition. We're moving from an industrial, physically oriented society to an abstract, invisible society. By that I mean we're dealing with data that's invisible. It's on a computer disc. We can't see it and we can't touch it. We're moving from a left-brain physical society to a right-brain abstract society.

Using Intuition in Decision Making

We've seen how innovators use intuition when spotting trends, working with people, and enhancing creativity. What about its role in decision making? We asked Fred Smith, chairman of Federal Express, to give his assessment:

> It's got to be half, because most people have an inherent resistance to "kaleidoscope thinking." They tend to judge the future as an extrapolation of the past. Maybe it's more comfortable that way. But if you want to innovate, you have to be capable of making intuitive judgments. Most people who innovate have this enormous thirst for information. What they're trying to do is hedge their bets. Really, intuition is not so much intuition as the amalgamation of a lot of stuff from a lot of different places which leads you to say, "Okay, it's a safe bet. It's not a fool's bet."

Managers who make it to the top constantly use intuition in decision making. But how well? Regis McKenna, who has helped dozens of high-tech companies think fundamentally about their markets and products, is an outspoken advocate of the power of intuition. He believes in informing your intuition by getting out in the marketplace and talking to your customer group:

> You have to immerse yourself in the environment. When I went into consulting for Apple, I spent a lot of time talking to people. I talked to dealers, I talked to analysts, I talked to users. I spent a lot of time really sitting in the environment and in fact dealing with small businesses. I can just walk around my own shop and see how people think about or what they're doing with computers, or not doing with computers, or what their fears are.

Intuitive knowledge, McKenna believes, is largely gained through experience, "and it's a safer way of understanding what is going on than rational, logical, linear synthesis."

McKenna uses the personal computer market as an example. In the early 1980s, statistics seemed to show that the industry was going to be $150 billion in the next ten years. The charts were going off the top of the page. Many companies decided that they needed to be in the retail business. As a result, as many as 150 companies jumped into the personal computer market with a product. But, as McKenna explains, they forgot something.

> They didn't talk to the retailers. If they had, they would have found out that the retail business itself was really just maturing and growing, that the salesperson in the store could only absorb an understanding of a limited number of machines, that standards were being set by people like IBM, that the channels in effect were very narrow. But all they looked at was the *quantitative* measurement. They didn't understand the *qualitative* factors that killed them. We have gotten so oriented toward quantitative measurement, when real entrepreneurs and real successful people have always made their decisions on an intuitive basis. You can only measure what you can control. You can't control the future.

Four Powerful Techniques for Enhancing Intuition

You may already know how tuned in you are to your intuition. If you're highly intuitive, what follows will provide you with additional insights. If you sense you need to further develop your intuitive powers, this section will provide some pointers.

Of course, awakening your intuition can't be broken down into a set of simple steps to follow. That's not the way it works. Nevertheless, what follows are some areas to look at and some things to think about that may help you increase your intuitive awareness.

1. Try to determine how your intuitive impulses feel. Intuitive knowing can come to you physically, mentally, emotionally, spiritually, or visually. The innovators in our study often mentioned physical or emotional sensations.

Laurel Burch, the San Francisco jewelry and clothing designer, feels it physically when she has a good idea:

> It's a full feeling, as opposed to a fragmented feeling. And there isn't any conflict within myself. If it's right and it's in alignment with my vision, then this feeling sort of fills me up. And if I have an idea that I'm uncertain about, then I seem to hear words of caution in my head urging me to rethink.

In 1979, entrepreneur Doug Greene sold a thriving magazine advertising sales business in Malibu, California, to follow a hunch that the natural foods industry needed a more comprehensive trade magazine. Greene, like Burch, receives intuitive directions physically—in the gut, to be exact:

> If I don't feel good in my stomach about a decision, I don't care if the numbers say we're going to make a jillion dollars, that's how important intuition is to me. It's an actual feeling either way. When it doesn't feel good, it's just like a stomachache or a nervous stomach. And when a decision feels right, it's like a great meal. It just feels good.

2. Strive to develop your self-awareness. "Self-awareness is the ground from which intuition comes to full fruition," notes Frances Vaughan in her excellent book *Awakening Intuition*. Awareness, as we have seen, is a key ingredient of the innovation process. To see ourselves as others see us, to know our strengths as well as our weaknesses, to confront our fears, to consciously realize the psychological "baggage" we carry from

141

our past, and to strive to unburden ourselves of limitations and prejudices—these are the requirements for becoming self-aware.

Increasing self-awareness is an ongoing process, a journey rather than a destination. There are many obstacles. The enemies of your self-awareness are shallow people who, if you spend enough time in their presence, will unwittingly convince you that genuine people don't exist. The enemy of your self-awareness is excessive emphasis on acquiring material things, at the expense of taking the time to build lasting and loving relationships. It is entirely possible to live your life without confronting who you really are; indeed, in Modern America all the "support systems" are in place for you to accomplish this with ease.

Innovators don't allow shallow people to dominate their lives. They avoid superficial, phony situations. They refuse to get sucked in by the *People* magazine/"Entertainment Tonight"/*National Enquirer* hype that so pervades current popular culture and mass media. We have asserted throughout this book that innovators adapt to change. But they also reject certain media-created fads and fashions.

There are many ways to aid the process of self-discovery. Reading books about consciousness and spirituality can point the way; the Bible is the book of self-discovery par excellence. Other activities such as quiet contemplation, running, attending seminars, and similar activities can help you to confront who you are and where you have come from. They help you to strengthen your resolve to create the future you want for yourself. Another avenue toward increasing self-awareness is to take time off from your career to devote to the study of thinking. This is an opportunity you'll have to create for yourself. Other suggestions: Spend a weekend at a prayer or meditation retreat, attend church if you don't regularly do so.

Concentrating on increasing your self-understanding and awareness is necessary to finding your internal guidance system. Sensitive, alert, confident, self-actualized individuals have a decided advantage in this era of change, complexity, and competition. They absorb more, perceive more, and retain more, all of which informs their intuition. When something "doesn't feel right," they quickly spot it.

3. Give yourself plenty of dream space. Management author Tom Peters has a rule: He doesn't work on weekends. He won't accept engagements that require him to fly on Sundays. Instead, he romps around on his New Hampshire farm or at his home in Palo Alto, California. President Reagan likes to retreat to his Santa Barbara ranch to chop wood and mend fences. And Lee Iacocca has said he works weekends only during crises. What do these leaders know about themselves from which the rest of us could benefit?

The answer isn't hard to figure out: The more intense your work, the more you need relaxation. The more decisions you make, the more good ideas you need to develop. Part of creating new ideas is using your intuition. A relaxed state of mind allows your subconscious mind to make the subtle connections required to generate new possibilities.

Yet as the number of demands on our leisure time increases, we are putting aside less and less time for quiet reflection, or what novelist Saul Bellow called "dream space." Are you always on the go? If so, chances are you are slighting the creativity-enhancing, intuition-spawning benefits of sitting quietly and doing nothing. If you feel you have no time left to call your own, you are vulnerable to stress, burnout, and an apathy that allows you to start believing you are doing everything you can to create the reality you want. When this mind-set takes over, you're stuck in the Victim Mode.

If you lack dream space, take action now to create some of it.

143

Review the priorities you set in chapter 2—several times a day. Next, examine everything you're currently involved in with an eye toward how it relates to your priorities. Streamline your activities and lessen your obligations.

We all face choices about how to spend our time. These small decisions add up to big ones. For example, if you've just had a busy week, maybe attending that weekend seminar *isn't* the best way to marshal your intuitive resources. What may be needed is some quiet time to think over your recent experiences and to think through coming events. Attending a seminar is a "new information" function; you'd be packing more new data into your computer. Hiking in the woods, working in the garden, or lying in the backyard hammock are all activities that give the mind a chance to mull over and "digest" the information and experiences you've already taken in.

Doug Greene, the natural-foods entrepreneur and chairman of New Hope Communications, today publishes a variety of trade and consumer newspapers and magazines. He remains a firm believer in the power of intuition. Greene grew up poor in Arkansas, worked his way through college driving a truck, and became an advertising sales rep, which eventually led to his own advertising sales firm. By the time he was twenty-five, Greene was a wealthy man. He had an ocean-front home in Malibu, several sports cars, and all the accoutrements of material success. But he wasn't happy.

On vacation in Mexico, Greene and his wife met a physician who told them about the health-enhancing powers of natural foods. The Greenes completely changed their diet and began reassessing their "fast lane" careers. In 1979, after a year of personal experimentation with natural foods, they decided to start *Natural Foods Merchandiser,* a trade magazine for natural-foods retailers. From this metamorphosis, Greene began other publications, including the highly successful *Delicious!,* as well as sponsoring a natural-foods trade show. In 1984, shortly after the U.S. invasion of Grenada, Greene went there as a private citizen to assess the situation. When he returned to the States, he organized the American Corps of Entrepreneurs and enlisted other entrepreneurs to fly down to Grenada to put on a two-day seminar for the Grenadians on how to rebuild their economy by starting small businesses.

Greene believes in the power of relaxation:

> I'm about ninety-five percent intuition-driven. I allow myself to listen to my intuition, to realize that there is a special voice inside that tells me special things. But the voice only talks to me when I'm in a state of relaxation.

Dream space is critical to tapping your intuition. It helps you to look at your problems in new ways. Being still is critical to quieting the mind, as Doug Greene has found when trying to make an important decision. He believes an important element in developing intuition is creating relaxing experiences on a regular basis:

> Once a month I schedule what I refer to as "Doug Days." From six o'clock one evening until nine o'clock the following day, I create a block of time where I have absolutely nothing to do. I have no appointments; I have an appointment every minute with *me.* I'll go to another city or to a different environment. And I'll sit and just draw or whatever my first instincts are to do. And I have to say that if I hadn't had those Doug Days the last year and a half, I wouldn't have nearly the business that I have, and I wouldn't have nearly the quality of life. Almost all the major innovations of my life in the last year and a half I can trace back to an idea that was born on a Doug Day.

4. Record your hunches in your idea notebook. As with your ideas, you may want to record your gut feelings and intuitive flashes in your idea notebook. This is one of the best ways to get in touch with your subconscious mind, and by writing down these flashes, you'll have a record of them for later reference. Do you feel strongly about something—some event that has yet to take place; some person you're considering entering into an alliance with? If so, try to determine what the feeling is based on.

Later, after the event has taken place, compare what you believed were intuitive feelings with what actually took place. If your intuitive feeling was accurate, try to remember when and how you became conscious of it. Try to recall as vividly as possible the feeling you experienced. Was it a physical sensation, a nervous stomach, perspiration, a vague feeling of "something fishy"?

If your hunch turns out to have been off the mark, try to identify the reason. Remember that intuition is almost always accurate. If your hunch was wrong, it probably wasn't intuition but guessing, projection, wishful thinking, or negative thinking. Nobody can hope to perfect his or her intuition to the point where it is correct all the time, but keeping a record of your hunches will help you identify truly intuitive insights.

Intuition and the New Era

As we were surveying the subject of intuition, we kept hearing that intuition is becoming indispensable as a coping tool in the new era.

"... humanity may be expected to transcend the present mental level and become more and more intuitive," writes Frances Vaughan.

"I think we're developing a real sixth sense to know and to sense and to see into the future," Doug Greene told us.

"Intuitive abilities will become more valuable during the coming period of surprises, complexities, and rapid changes," says Weston Agor, who has researched the use of intuition in business.

In *Reinventing the Corporation,* John Naisbitt says intuition will become "increasingly valuable in the new information society because there is so much data."

No doubt intuition will become more important than it already is. As society becomes more and more complex, intuition really does become an indispensable tool. Despite the return in the 1980s to fast-track living, the Baby Boom generation is still interested in maintaining a balanced life-style that leaves room for contemplation, concentration, and dream space. In the minds of people who value balance, intuition flourishes. They use experience to teach and to inform their intuition. They believe that complexity, competition, and change *can* be managed.

Begin right now to change the way you respond to your inner voice. And remember that intuition works best when it is fed with high-quality information and ideas, and the desire to find and exploit opportunities. This orientation to opportunities and how you can improve your ability to spot them is the subject of the next chapter.

PART III
Implementing Your Innovations

EIGHT

Spotting Opportunities in Change

**In my book, if you're not number one,
you've got to innovate.**

Lee Iacocca

So far in this book, we've examined the innovator's thinking skills. Now it's time to bring those skills to bear upon specific tasks. In this chapter we'll show you how innovators use their thinking skills to discover major, turning-point opportunities.

A major theme of this chapter is that most successful innovations exploit change—in people's attitudes, in demographics, in technology, and so forth. So first let's look at how one innovator discovers opportunities in change and then at five sources you can turn to for innovative opportunities of your own.

In the Innovation Age it is dangerous to assume that we'll have the same opportunities tomorrow as we do today. Those who assume their employer will continue to create the opportunities to justify their employment may find themselves considered a "cost" rather than a "resource." Spotting opportunities in change is an important skill of the new era, and it's one of the Secret Skills of innovators. Indeed, all of us must become opportunity spotters if we want to thrive and prosper today. Creating new opportunities must be viewed as an ongoing activity, both in your role as an employee and as president of YOU, INC.

Pause for a moment to consider: What is your next Breakthrough Idea? What do you consider your next big project, directional shift, or life change? Your spontaneous mental response to these questions may be revealing. If you are satisfied with your present job, "Breakthrough Idea" probably starts you thinking about a new project for the company. If you are *not* satisfied, Breakthrough Idea might conjure up a personal project or goal. Either way, the ability to spot opportunities in change can be helpful.

Innovators are hardly the only individuals who are opportunity-oriented. But what makes them uniquely valuable as role models is their ability to be among the first to realize the significance of a change. Let's observe how one of them does it.

Stuart Karl: Master Opportunity Spotter

Stuart Karl, chairman of Karl • Lorimar Home Video, consistently recognizes trends and builds opportunities based on them. What can we learn from him that will help us? To answer this question, let's first look at his accomplishments to date.

Karl grew up in Newport Beach, California, an affluent, rapidly growing community south of Los Angeles. While his friends spent their summers surfing or working in their fathers' firms, Stuart preferred to make it on his own. At seventeen, Karl had his first Breakthrough Idea.

In fun-loving Southern California, fads and fashions seemed to appear with the frequency of the tides. One of these fads was the waterbed. As it happened, Newport Beach had no waterbed dealer. Karl got to know a dealer in Hollywood, from whom he purchased frameless waterbeds at thirty dollars apiece. Back in Newport he ran a classified ad in the local paper to sell waterbeds for fifty-five dollars each. The strategy worked fine until some of the waterbeds leaked, and Karl began receiving complaints from irate customers in the middle of the night. He stopped selling them.

During his short stint as a waterbed salesman, Karl noticed that waterbed retailers were without a trade magazine. Karl's family lived next door to Bud Knapp, owner of *Architectural Digest* and *Bon Appetit,* and to Stuart, publishing seemed like a good business. A second Breakthrough Idea occurred: Why not start such a magazine? "One of the first people I tried to sell an ad to asked to see my rate card," Karl told us. "I had never heard of a rate card before." It didn't matter. The first issue of *Industry* magazine, laid out with grease pencil, tape, and glue in Karl's bedroom, netted a profit of eight hundred dollars.

As the waterbed industry took off, so did *Industry* magazine. But Karl wasn't satisfied with just one magazine. Soon he spotted opportunity in the hot tubs and spas bubbling in the backyards of Southern California homes. Before long he had launched *Spa* and *Sauna.*

Next Karl bought up several weekly newspapers in the

Newport area and kept his eye open for additional magazine concepts. Noticing the rising popularity of city magazines such as *New West* and *New York,* Karl started *Orange Coast* for booming Orange County. After purchasing a VCR in 1978, he noticed that video rental shops were without a trade magazine. Shortly thereafter he launched *Video Store.*

Despite his success Karl became bored with publishing and began looking for opportunities elsewhere. He spotted one in the VCR, and in 1979 he sold off his publications in preparation for his biggest launch ever.

The first VCR came on the market in the mid-1970s and the average cost was fifteen hundred dollars. By 1979, the price had dipped below twelve hundred dollars, and sales were starting to take off. Not only that, the technology was improving: The newer VCRs were less bulky and easier to operate. Karl saw that it wouldn't be long before millions of Americans owned one. The VCR, he began to see, was destined to become an appliance.

In publishing *Video Store,* Karl had become familiar with the available programming. All the video rental shops stocked were movies and X-rated entertainment. What struck Karl was the fact that bookstores were full of "how to" books: cookbooks, pop psychology books, exercise books, business books. In an increasingly complex "information" society, people constantly wanted (indeed *needed*) to know how to do new things, and "how to" books accounted for the bulk of bookstore sales. The video industry, mired in its own groupthink, saw itself exclusively as an entertainment industry. Putting these disparate thoughts and observations together, Karl hatched his next Breakthrough Idea: Why not expand the viewer's choice by adapting some of the "how to" books to video?

Karl vividly recalls when the pieces of this idea suddenly came together:

I was visiting some friends who had a VCR, and for some reason they brought out the tape we were going to watch inside a hollow brown book cover instead of the box it came in. I looked at it and for a moment I thought it *was* a book. The idea hit me; I went bananas, saying, "This is it! This is publishing of the future!"

Perhaps because it was "publishing of the future," getting Karl Video off the ground was anything but easy. This time Karl was doing more than taking a familiar concept like trade magazines and applying it to new industries. Now he was in a new industry trying to create a whole new market niche.

At first, the company survived off royalties from sales of his magazines. The first two tapes he produced, *Exercise Now* and *Graham Kerr's Galloping Gourmet,* didn't exactly go platinum. Video retailers weren't interested, claiming that customers wanted only entertainment. "They thought I was a fool at the video trade shows," Karl recalled. "I remember people stopping by the booth and saying, 'Why would anybody want to watch someone learn how to do something when you can read about it? That's ridiculous.' " Nevertheless, Karl remained convinced his idea was a good one, if maybe a wee bit before its time. Video retailers, he believed, couldn't see that instructional tapes would find a market because customers didn't know they were available. And the public would know about them only if he could convince retailers to carry them.

Although the company continued losing money, Karl pressed on. He tried hundreds of new ideas to build his market. Simultaneously, he tried to find out what the market wanted. As experiments, he arranged with NBC to sell the last television interview with John Lennon. He made a video of Mike Wallace's television portrait of Marilyn Monroe. Neither were particularly profitable, although the Lennon interview made its way briefly onto the charts. He knew he still hadn't found the right product to sell. And then, well, you already know the rest of the story. One day Karl's wife, Deborah, having just read Jane Fonda's best-selling *Workout* exercise book, suggested he turn the book into a video. Not a bad idea, Karl admitted. The Breakthrough Idea became, "Get Jane Fonda to do it!"

But how? Again, Karl was moving in uncharted territory. No other star had made an exercise video before. How could he even get to Jane Fonda, much less convince her that she should sign with his tiny company?

With characteristic persistence, Karl searched for a way to turn the idea into a reality. Through his contacts at NBC, he learned that RCA was also seeking video rights to *Workout*. Rather than compete with RCA, Karl decided to join them. In doing so, he had more credibility when he approached Fonda. "I struck up a personal relationship with Jane," Karl said. "I told her we weren't going to make her one of a hundred tapes in our catalog, that she would be our top tape."

Karl guessed *Workout* might sell as many as twenty-five thousand copies. His estimate was a bit conservative. By 1986, *Workout* had sold over a million copies worldwide. Meanwhile, Karl Video had merged with Lorimar Telepictures, the giant entertainment concern. Karl • Lorimar Home Video now produces and distributes not only instructional videos but feature films, children's videos, and video magazines as well.

Stuart Karl's Little-Known Techniques

Stuart Karl has clearly established himself as someone able to spot and to take advantage of the opportunities change presents. Does he have any secrets? What is his own explanation for how he rode the Wave again and again?

A lot of people have asked me that question. And as much as I don't like to say it, so much of it was just luck. I really have no way to tell you how I did it. Waterbeds have gone from being a hippie deal to being flotation sleep systems used by hospitals and sold at Sears. Spas are now all over the world and they're not just these funky hot tubs; they're in all the health centers. But I've got to tell you, waterbeds, spas, VCRs—with all of them it was like one day they were just there and it all crystallized. I was not looking for a waterbed gig. I was just looking to get into something exciting.

It was a simple, honest appraisal, and one that should have satisfied us. But it didn't. How could one person have so much luck? As we probed further, we discovered that Stuart Karl does what every other innovator does who finds opportunities in change.

1. Stuart Karl is an active observer of change. He subscribes to seventy magazines and newspapers a month! He is a voracious reader of both consumer and trade magazines, newsletters, and nonfiction books. In a sitting area of his spacious office is a five-foot-high pile of recent newspapers: the *Washington Post, Women's Wear Daily,* the *Wall Street Journal.* Karl reads everything from *Manhattan, Inc.,* and *John Naisbitt's Trend Letter* to the most obscure dirt bike magazine and the *Political Eye.* After we broached the subject of his appetite to know what is going on in the wider world, Karl observed, "I've always been accused by my friends of reading too much. But for me one of the most fun things I do is to spend a weekend going back through old magazines. You just read and it's interesting."

2. Stuart Karl is idea-oriented. He is constantly coming up with ideas, proposing solutions to problems, and identifying possible new opportunities. During our interview, at one point he jumped up to jot down an idea. He estimated that he comes up with three or more possible Breakthrough Ideas per day, which he tests out on people.

3. Stuart Karl is opportunity-oriented. Said Court Shannon, executive vice-president at Karl • Lorimar, "No matter what you're talking about or what discussion is on the table, Stuart's mind is constantly pursuing and exploring coordinated possibilities that might result in either a new videotape project or a new business venture that might be successful. Even though he's with you and he's listening to exactly what you say, he's always keeping his mind rolling on other tangents that might be possible hot ventures."

Karl looks for opportunities in the information he loads into his mental files. He is constantly attempting to see patterns in the changes in society, whatever those changes are, and the sources of new opportunities. As Shannon puts it: "There are a lot of patterns out there but you have to be able to convert those into an applicable and marketable concept."

Finding Innovative Opportunities of Your Own

Stuart Karl is adept at sensing the direction of the Wave. With him, opportunity seeking is an instinctive process. But even if this pattern recognition doesn't come to you quite so naturally, you can train yourself to see the patterns as you go about observing trends, patterns that can tip you off to new opportunities. What follows are the five sources of innovative opportunities most often cited by the innovators in our study:

1. Observe a trend and come up with a way of exploiting it. Take the breakup of AT&T, for example. Literally hundreds of new companies have been spawned as a result of the federal court's ruling permitting competition. These include everything from independent long-distance telephone companies to alternative telephone-directory publishers.

One of the many companies to exploit this change was Corporate Telecomm, a Van Nuys, California, firm which counsels businesses on the type of phone systems they need, then sells and installs the necessary equipment. Company founder Todd Bernstein started the business as a hobby in 1980, when he was eighteen, teaching himself how to install phones by reading Pacific Telephone installation manuals found in the company's trash bins. Bernstein realized what a boom deregulation would be to his business and expanded to meet the increasing demand. By 1986, Corporate Telecomm employed eighteen people and had annual revenues of $1.5 million.

Seeking opportunity in change led Cartwright Sheppard to start an entirely different kind of service business. A Los Angeles stockbroker and investment advisor, Sheppard noticed an increase in the number of clients coming to him for advice about financial aid for their children's education. Sheppard began to see this unmet need arising from a number of sources:

- The cost of a college education was rising at a rate greater than the rate of inflation, at a time when the government was tightening eligibility requirements for student aid.
- Applying for financial aid, like filing a tax return, was becoming *increasingly complex* and the rules changed frequently.
- With more and more two-wage-earner families, parents had less time to familiarize themselves with the many sources of financial aid.

Looking at these changes, Sheppard saw opportunity. His Breakthrough Idea: "Start a financial counseling service that specialized in helping parents arrange financial aid for their children." In 1984, Sheppard and two partners opened their first College Center in Los Angeles. Two years later, College Center had become a franchise and is operating in three states.

Neither Corporate Telecomm nor College Centers took great amounts of capital to establish. But they both required someone to spot changes and to figure a way to exploit them. Bernstein and Sheppard were able to sense unmet needs brought about by changes in the environment. Both Bernstein and Sheppard happened to be in the entrepreneurial sector, but this same skill is useful in every sector of our society. The more adept you are at spotting changes and figuring ways to convert them into opportunities, the more in demand you'll be in the new era.

As you go about looking for signals of change in your daily life, take a moment to think about what opportunities (and threats) changes might mean, and to whom. For example, as the number of two-income households continues to rise, what opportunities might this change bring, and for whom? When the Campbell Soup Company asked this question, the answer was: "Us." They realized that working couples have less time to spend in the kitchen. But they didn't necessarily want to eat the available TV dinners, either. They wanted a more nutritious meal, and they were willing to pay more for it. As a result, Campbell introduced its Le Menu line of frozen dinners.

2. Search for solutions to negative trends. If you can identify negative trends and come up with a way to counteract them, you may have a Breakthrough Idea.

John Shea, a Memphis ear surgeon, could not help but notice the spiraling cost of health care. Shea realized that health care costs could not keep outpacing inflation indefinitely, and that an opportunity lay in discounting medical services. "If we continued on this course," Shea told us, "medical care would become so expensive that the country couldn't afford it. And then the government would intervene and impose a system like they have in England where everybody works for the government."

To Shea, that was no solution at all. As he began focusing on the problem, he saw that the way to reduce his patients' hospital costs was to eliminate the hospital since, as he puts it, "No amount of telling the hospitals that they ought to cut their prices is ever going to work." Shea's Breakthrough Idea was to replace the hospital with what he calls an "outpatient surgery center." The center is essentially a fully equipped clinic joined by enclosed passageways to a suite hotel where the patient can recover under the supervision of a trained nursing staff. Before and after operations, patients and their spouses stay in the adjoining hotel. Nursing care is provided as needed, but the patient doesn't have to pay for excess services he or she doesn't require, as in the typical hospital. Shea's first center opened in 1985 in Memphis, and already Shea Clinic is mapping plans to expand. He sees applications in other areas too, such as orthopedics and ophthalmology.

Pinpoint a negative trend and ask: What will happen if this continues? What can you do to provide the affected customer group with an alternative solution?

Consider the "trend" of growing budget deficits and rising pressure to cut government spending. One solution that is receiving an increasing amount of interest in the mid-1980s is privatization, whereby government services (garbage collection, emergency services, street maintenance) are performed by private, for-profit companies. Companies set up to provide these "government" services are thriving because they can provide services for less than the government agencies. As government budget deficits continue to mount, privatization will probably continue. How might this become an opportunity for you or your company?

If you are a farmer and you see a trend toward greater reliance on ecologically destructive fertilizers and pesticides, you might question where this trend leads. Is there a better way of growing crops? When innovator William Thompson asked himself this question, it started him on a path of discovery that eventually led him to design a completely different method of farming, as we shall see in chapter 9.

3. Look at your current activities, beliefs, and interests for ideas that might appeal to others. Some innovative ideas exploit change in an accidental way. Certain innovators start a business because it "feels like it might have potential" or because they believe in it themselves. Suddenly it takes off.

This happened to Mo Siegel, co-founder of Celestial Seasonings Herbal Tea Company. Before Siegel came along, there was only one kind of tea—black tea. In 1971, Siegel began introducing America to Red Zinger, Sleepytime, Mellow Mint, and Mandarin Orange Spice. When Celestial Seasonings was first founded, it consisted of Siegel, his partner John Hay, and a few friends. Driving their beat-up Datsun, Siegel and his wife, Peggy, sold herb tea to health-food stores from California to New England. In a matter of two years, they had trouble keeping up with demand.

Celestial Seasonings capitalized on the health-and-fitness trend. Herb teas are caffeine-free, and thus appeal to growing numbers of health-conscious Americans looking for a coffee substitute. But capitalizing on the health trend wasn't what motivated Siegel to try the tea business.

"John Hay and I were basically just looking for something to do," Siegel explained. As manager of a health food store in Aspen, Colorado, Siegel noticed an increase in the popularity of the peppermint and comfrey teas the store sold. He'd sampled both and wasn't wild about the taste of either. An avid hiker and backpacker, Siegel began collecting herbs in the Colorado countryside. He would then blend different herbs together, hoping to improve the flavor. "I figured if you could make the stuff taste good, you'd have an idea," he recalls.

Siegel made the stuff taste good. His blends are a trade secret. But he did more than blend tea. He recognized the Wave he had happened upon and marketed his new product in creative ways. He packaged herb teas in brightly colored boxes with beautiful pictures on them. He marketed his teas not just to health food stores but to supermarkets and restaurants as well. He spent millions to advertise herb teas in mainstream magazines with the slogan "soothing teas for a nervous world." Six years after founding Celestial Seasonings, Siegel was a millionaire. In 1984, he sold Celestial Seasonings to Kraft, Inc.

Dean Kamen, the medical technologist we heard about in chapter 1, knew that his invention of a miniature pump solved a problem for a particular customer group (research doctors). As soon as a medical journal made mention of its availability, he began receiving calls from researchers around the world. Kamen's response was to start a business to make more pumps. Over the next five years he continued to perfect his designs. He also began looking for customer groups which might benefit from his pump. The result was that he began making portable insulin pumps for diabetics.

Like Siegel and Kamen, you may already be in the middle of an opportunity. Your next Breakthrough Idea may come from looking around at your current activities, interests, hobbies, and beliefs. Ask yourself these questions: What am I doing that could serve a larger group? What unexpected successes have I had? What might they mean?

4. When a present trend is running against you, come up with a new idea. Recognizing a threat is half the battle. It may also be the source of a Breakthrough Idea.

Al Neuharth, chairman and CEO of Gannett Company,

Inc., didn't like the handwriting on the wall. He was observing an apparent death cycle among newspapers across the nation. The trend had intensified in the late seventies and early eighties. Gone were such papers as the *Washington Star,* the *Philadelphia Bulletin,* the *Cleveland Press,* and the *Minneapolis Star.* Neuharth recognized that life-style changes were responsible for the demise of these afternoon papers. Instead of reading the paper, Americans watched television news when they came home at night. In addition, a widening array of special-interest magazines gave readers in-depth discussions of the issues that most concerned them. Given the higher costs of publishing, many communities could no longer support a local newspaper with advertising revenues. Increasingly, the local paper was little more than a collection of wire-service dispatches and reports of the latest murders and political scandals.

Looking at these changes, Neuharth and his team discovered developments that could be turned into an exciting new opportunity for Gannett: a national daily newspaper. For one thing, America was becoming a more homogeneous society. Neuharth noted the huge increase in television viewing and in the number of people who reported that they were getting their news from television. He also noticed millions of Americans were flying, which meant they wanted to know the weather in other cities. And he saw that satellite technology, which already enabled the *Wall Street Journal* to be a national daily newspaper, would allow him to transfer color layouts less expensively and more rapidly than in the past. He put all of these factors together and came up with a Breakthrough Idea: *USA Today.*

Similarly, Lewis Lapham of *Harper's* realized that the venerable magazine he edited was in need of a change. This realization came, he told us, not by looking at its dismal financial shape (it was losing $1.5 million a year) but by "an intuitive sensing on my part that the magazine had become irrelevant." He continues:

> I could go around and talk to people and they would say, "Oh, yes, *Harper's Magazine*. Isn't that nice?" And even those who looked at it couldn't quote from it. It was clear that our readers really weren't reading the magazine; they just felt they ought to subscribe, because they felt guilty about spending so much of their time watching "Monday Night Football" instead of reading self-improving texts. People were reading the [opinion] pages of the big newspapers, or *Time,* or watching the networks. People would go to cocktail parties and they'd talk about what Kissinger said on "Nightline" or about what somebody wrote on the [opinion] page of the *Washington Post* or the *New York Times*. The magazine was becoming more and more like homework for an examination that nobody ever gave.

More important, Lapham himself had grown bored with editing *Harper's*. Even he didn't enjoy reading it anymore. The reason, he suggests, was that there weren't enough good articles to be found each month, because there weren't that many good magazine writers; there was no money in writing for magazines anymore. "The people who would have been into magazine writing twenty-five years ago and could have made a living at it can't anymore—so they're going to be writing, if they're literate, screenplays or corporate speeches or books."

Lapham decided that the venerable magazine needed a change. But when he approached the *Harper's Magazine* Foundation to get approval, he was turned down. He resigned. Two years later, as the magazine's prospects continued to deteriorate, Lapham was reinstated. Wasting no time, he created a section of articles excerpted from a wide variety of sources: books, screenplays, longer magazine articles, court transcripts, Senate testimony, short opinion-type essays, radio transcripts, and newsletters. He added the *Harper's* Index, a compilation of interesting and/or informative statistics ("percentage of unemployed Americans who receive no unemployment benefits: 75"). And he created the monthly Forum, which brings together groups of opinion leaders to discuss topics ranging from urban crime to the future of literacy in America.

Lewis Lapham saw that the trends were running against *Harper's Magazine.* He reacted by creating a new format. As a result, subscriptions are up at *Harper's* and the deficit is down.

Look at your worst problems for possible Breakthrough Ideas. Where have you noticed handwriting on the wall? What ideas can you come up with to counteract it?

5. Watch what the competition is doing, and do it better. All business innovators come to realize this idea, whether it's Don Burr in airlines, Fred Smith in freight delivery, Ray Kroc in hamburgers, or Sandy Gooch in natural foods.

Schoolteacher Sandy Gooch didn't set out to beat the competition, or even to capitalize on the health-and-fitness trend. Her Breakthrough Idea came about as the result of a close brush with death.

It started with a case of the sniffles that wouldn't go away. Gooch's doctor prescribed tetracycline, a common antibiotic. A few days later she found herself shaking, her head spinning. When she was admitted to a hospital, doctors could not find anything wrong. Two weeks later, Gooch's doctor again prescribed tetracycline, this time for an eye infection. Within minutes, she suffered another even more violent seizure. Her muscles quivered uncontrollably. Her heart pounded. Her chest tightened.

166

This time she was rushed one hundred miles south to the Scripps Institute in La Jolla, California. A team of specialists examined her, but they could not figure out the cause of her seizures. As before, her symptoms gradually subsided. Then on the fifth day Gooch took a sip of diet soda. Suddenly, her body was again thrown into the same violent convulsions, only worse. The attack was so violent that she stopped breathing. A nurse, realizing that her life was in danger, injected a shot of Benadryl, a powerful antihistamine. The attack subsided, although she remained gravely ill.

A week later Gooch was released, the cause of her outbreaks as much a mystery as before. Weak and depressed, she lived with the fear that something she ate might bring on yet another attack. She went to bed each night not knowing if she would wake up the next morning. Her days were filled with doctor visits and referrals to still other doctors, but none of them could help her. One doctor, in total frustration, told her, "It's all in your head."

Gooch credits her father with saving her life. A research biologist and chemist, he became convinced that her outbreaks were caused by chemical additives in processed food. He encouraged her to adopt a diet of natural foods: No refined flour or sugar. No artificial additives. No artificial flavors, colors, or preservatives. No caffeine. No hydrogenated vegetable oil. Gooch took his advice and gradually regained her health.

During her recovery, Gooch began reading book after book on nutrition, health, and foods. While shopping at health food stores, she noticed that not all of them had the same standards. Some even sold products with sugar and additives in them. In addition, the stores she shopped at were small, making it necessary to go one place for fresh vegetables, another for staples, another for meat, and to a conventional supermarket for light bulbs and such.

It was then that Gooch's Breakthrough Idea occurred: Why not start a natural food supermarket, with everything else offered by regular grocery stores available as well? In 1977, using her teacher-retirement money and personal savings, she opened the first Mrs. Gooch's Natural Food Store. Nine years later, there are six markets in the Los Angeles area and the company does over $40 million in sales annually.

Sandy Gooch's Breakthrough Idea came about from noticing what other health food stores were doing—and then doing it better. She has taken the natural food store beyond the "mom and pop" size and put it on a par with chain operations. At Mrs. Gooch's, the customer can find naturally grown beef, organically grown produce, and food that contains no artificial additives or preservatives. The health-conscious customer doesn't have to take time to read labels. The selection, based on strict criteria, has already taken place in the buying office, before the food products reach the shelves.

Discovering Your Breakthrough Idea

Breakthrough Ideas are most likely to occur when you are calmly, confidently searching for new opportunities. They often appear after lengthy periods of thought and consideration. They occur to those who are prepared to *act*. Rather than a single magical moment in which the idea arrives, fully developed, you may find that your next Breakthrough Idea comes to you in pieces; pieces you must gradually put together.

However they come to you, all Breakthrough Ideas "check out" from various angles: They solve someone's problem; they satisfy a want; they are right for *you*. A Breakthrough Idea must align with your values and with your vision of your life. You will recognize it intuitively.

We could write many more words about the process of discovering Breakthrough Ideas. Instead, we are including a short list of questions designed to summarize what we have learned from innovators. Use it to stimulate your thinking.

1. What can I offer that "they" aren't offering?
2. How can I position myself in a way that is different?
3. Where's the niche that hasn't been developed?
4. How can I *add value* to the service or product I now produce?
5. Where is the market inefficiency?
6. What would make this process or procedure more convenient?
7. How can I do this less expensively?
8. What would people pay for that isn't available now?
9. What might my customer group want if it were available?
10. What do I really enjoy doing that I'd like to do more of?
11. How can I make a living from doing what to me is fun, challenging, and never boring?
12. What trends will change the assumptions my colleagues and competitors are presently making about my field?
13. What's next for YOU, INC?

If you've followed the suggestions set out in this chapter, you may already be toying with some potential Breakthrough Ideas. If so, your next question is this: How do I turn this idea into a reality? As we'll discover in the next chapter, innovators have developed special techniques to accomplish this task.

NINE

Building Your Breakthrough Idea

Everyone who's ever taken a shower has had an idea.
It's the person who gets out of the shower, dries off,
and does something about it who makes a difference.

Nolan Bushnell
Founder of Atari

Bill Reed, an elementary school vice-principal, wasn't satisfied with the financial rewards of his job. He wanted to do something that would utilize his teaching and administrative skills, as well as allow him to be his own boss.

One day it occurred to Reed (whose name we changed to protect his privacy) that many students suffered academically because of poor reading skills. Reading was not supported in many homes. Elementary-school kids were watching television in their off-hours. Reading was viewed as a chore, something to do only if it were assigned. How could he solve this problem and create an opportunity for himself at the same time?

Reed saw that the only way children could improve reading skills was by reading for pleasure. This would have to come outside regular school hours and would require the cooperation of parents. But parents often felt they couldn't help because they didn't know what books to buy.

Putting these observations together, Bill hit upon a Breakthrough Idea: Why not hold seminars for parents on the importance of encouraging their kids to read? In these seminars, he would persuade parents of the importance of reading to academic success and offer tips on how to get children to read more. Reed concluded that the best place to hold his seminars was in hotel conference rooms rather than school auditoriums. He had attended introductory seminars on speed reading and real estate investing and seen how popular they were. Even though he would charge a small admission fee, Reed felt parents would surely attend. In addition, he could make money by selling quality children's books in the back of the room. He believed he could get parents so fired up about reading that they would buy thousands of dollars worth of books to take home to their kids.

The idea was a sure thing, he decided. It was just the kind of opportunity he was looking to create. He was certain he could make a profit. He imagined himself becoming a nationally recognized authority on reading.

Reed decided to implement his idea right away. He located a company that sold mailing lists. He rented a conference room at a local hotel. He had an instructional packet printed up. He designed a flyer with his picture on it and sent it out. And he practiced his speech.

Twenty-three people showed up. There were enough seats for a hundred. As Bill Reed looked out over the rows of empty seats, he could barely conceal his disappointment. Afterward, the participants browsed through the books displayed at the back of the room, but bought few. His losses totalled fifty-five hundred dollars. He never held another seminar.

Where did I go wrong? What should I have done differently? Reed asked himself. Familiar questions. In fact, most of us have probably asked these questions about our own ideas, after things didn't go as planned. We hatched what seemed like a brilliant idea. We felt sure it was a winner. We knew we could pull it off. But everything went wrong. And like Bill Reed we wondered, was the idea flawed or was it the way we went about it?

Between coming up with an idea and deciding to implement it, there is an interim stage. During this "prelaunch" period, you think through the idea, build and refine it, try to anticipate the worst, and figure out how to make the idea a reality. Mastering this stage is the subject of this chapter. Innovators have much to teach us about building Breakthrough Ideas before launching them. For them, this is a process that combines both *thinking* skills and *doing* skills. This process keeps them from acting on weak ideas and prevents false starts. From their experiences, we have culled four key steps to successfully building a Breakthrough Idea.

Step 1: Avoid Premature Closure

You're a bit obsessed with your idea. You can't get it out of your mind. It represents everything you want for yourself and those around you: new opportunity, advancement, greater success and recognition.

At this stage it requires real effort to remain open to the possibility that your idea isn't feasible. Your obsession can blind you to its flaws and to the possibility that it isn't doable right now.

Remind yourself often that you are investigating this idea, not trying to defend it. You are trying to figure out if the idea is doable and whether or not it is the right one for you. During this stage your mind-set should be one of openness and alertness. You must be open to new information and contradictory viewpoints. You must be willing to have your prejudices exposed and your assumptions challenged. And you must be alert to trends and environmental changes that could negatively affect the viability of your idea. It is particularly important to pay attention to your intuition. Did the idea seem stronger when it first occurred to you? Or does it become stronger the more you develop it?

By being open and alert, you avoid what pay-television pioneer Rinaldo Brutoco calls "premature closure." You're holding your decision in abeyance for a while. Wayne Silby, the financial-services innovator, calls this period "the dance." He lets his mind "rock 'n' roll" with the idea. "The more important the decision, the bigger the idea, the longer I like to do the dance," Silby says. During this stage you're not trying to talk yourself out of acting on the idea, nor are you trying to sell yourself on it. If and when you do decide to launch the idea, you'll commit your full energies to making it work. But for now, *neutral* is the word. There is more to be done before you commit to launch.

Step 2: Gather Strategic Information

To build and test your idea, you need "Strategic Information"—specialized, solution-based, state-of-the-art knowledge, data, and informed opinion. Strategic Information enables you to know how—indeed *whether*—to implement your idea.

Innovators understand the role of information in the new era. For most of history, political scientist Leon Martel points out in his book *Mastering Change,* human labor was society's principal "transforming" resource, meaning it was the application of muscle power that created goods of value. Gradually human labor was replaced with a new transforming resource: energy. And in the new era (which Martel refers to as "postindustrial society") he notes that information is rapidly replacing energy as society's main transforming resource. Yet in contrast to human labor or energy, both of which are depleted by use, information can be used again and again. The problem lies in finding that information.

> *One of the greatest challenges of the Innovation Age is gaining access to information we need, when we need it. Thus, Strategic Information becomes crucial, for it enables us to act.*

Because of the information explosion, all of us must take into account more information to make decisions. Look at how often the word *research* enters our conversations. Buying a new car? Better do some research. Consult *Consumer Reports* to see what it says about that make and model. We rely upon information so often that we spend a great deal of our personal and company budgets buying information. We hire others to gather it for us. For instance, our tax preparer gathers information about current tax laws and loopholes. We could do it ourselves, but we would rather leverage this time-consuming task. At work, the management consultant provides information we could find ourselves—if we had the time.

Information is a precious resource. Unlike other resources, this one can be free if you know how to find it. Understanding how to gather Strategic Information is one of the Secret Skills of innovators. Their appetite for learning about things not immediately useful and their interest in knowing a little bit about everything comes in handy when they need facts. Innovators are relentless in the pursuit of information. If the information exists, they will find it. If it doesn't, they will compile it.

How does this relate to you? To innovate, you must increase your resourcefulness in bringing information to bear on the issues raised by your Breakthrough Idea. Two questions will face you immediately.

1. What information do I need to determine whether or not this idea is feasible? If your idea is to open a new frozen yogurt shop, for example, you might want to list such questions as: Is frozen yogurt becoming more or less popular? What is the best location? What is it like to run a retail shop? How do the best frozen yogurt shops operate? What ideas can I borrow from them? What ideas from other retail businesses could I apply to mine? How could I add value to such a shop? What is a good name for my shop?

Keep adding questions to your list as they occur. When you discuss your idea with others, they're bound to raise new possibilities. Take their suggestions seriously and add them to your list.

2. How do I find the information I need? This is where risk taking comes in. Sometimes you must pick up the phone and call perfect strangers. The only real risk you take is in being rebuffed. The response you expect is, "What, you're taking up my time to ask me such a question? How dare you?" But most of the time people with information are happy to share it, if you approach them with respect. They do the same thing when they need information.

How long should your Strategic Information gathering take? That depends on your idea. Before Robert Giaimo, the Washington, D.C., restaurateur, decided what his first American Cafe should look like, or what its cuisine should be, he spent much time gathering information. He had operated a Blimpie's franchise while attending Georgetown University, and upon graduation, he was ready to start a restaurant of his own. As Giaimo told us, "I wanted to do something innovative, something that represented my own creativity, something that was our own company, something that we could build from scratch and take national, and something that we could really be proud of."

Giaimo and his partners thought their Strategic Information-gathering phase would take about two months. It took two years. They traveled around the country, tasting, eating, and talking to restaurant owners. "We excited the energies of leaders in the food world," says Giaimo, "people like James Beard and Joe Baum, the food critics. They sparked our creative energies and we went further."

What they discovered was that American restaurants tended to gravitate toward two ends of a spectrum: fast food at one end and fine dining at the other. In between there were coffee shops. "We felt coffee shops were out-of-date, that they were part of the Howard Johnson's era and not the future," says Giaimo. "Nobody was really serving the middle price range with high-quality American casual fare. To us, freshness was important; taste was important; and most of all, *American* was important. We observed that not by looking at what was happening with food trends but with political trends. The whole 'back to basics' movement was afoot in the country at that time. And it was out of this information-gathering process that we started American Cafe."

Giaimo's two-year information-gathering journey may seem a bit excessive. But it's just the kind of thing innovators do. They are obsessed with finding the available information and mastering it as it relates to their idea. They are incredibly resourceful in uncovering the information they need to do what they want to do.

Step 3: Borrow and Combine Ideas

Breakthrough Ideas are seldom new ones. They are usually existing ideas brought together in a novel way.

Don Burr, chairman and founder of People Express, perceived an unmet need that other airlines were content to ignore: There were many more Americans who wanted to fly than could afford to. He saw deregulation of the airlines in 1978 as an opportunity. His Breakthrough Idea: Start a discount airline. The idea behind People Express is that the airplane seat is a commodity, just like a can of tennis balls or a barrel of oil. If you provide the passenger with a less expensive seat, you expand his choices and you increase the number of people who can afford to fly.

In order to reduce the cost of operations, Burr skillfully combined a number of existing ideas in a way that revolutionized an industry. People Express was not the first airline to discount fares. PSA (Pacific Southwest Airlines) had done so as far back as the early 1960s. People Express was not the first airline to go without frills. Laker's Skytrains had pioneered "no frills" treatment on transatlantic flights between London and New York. Nor were Burr's management ideas all that new. Numerous high-tech firms were experimenting with innovative management methods to increase productivity.

Or if we look at the accomplishments of Mitchell Kapor, the innovator who revolutionized personal-computer software, we find the same thing at work: an ability to borrow ideas and combine them in a way that better serves the needs of the customer group.

Kapor's Breakthrough Idea, a brand of spread-sheet software called Lotus 1-2-3, enables personal-computer operators to analyze numbers in minutes that would take weeks if done by hand. Released in 1982, the software zoomed to the top of sales charts, where it has remained. It made Kapor an instant multimillionaire at age thirty-two when Lotus Development Corporation went public the following year. Nevertheless, Lotus 1-2-3 was not the first spread-sheet software. That distinction goes to VisiCalc, produced by a company called VisiCorp, where Kapor had worked briefly as a computer programmer.

What Kapor did was combine a number of ideas that already existed. He used the ideas in VisiCalc's spread-sheet software and combined them with a program that could form graphs from spread-sheet numbers. And he added a data-base management system to 1-2-3 that made it possible to keep inventory on the personal computer.

Kapor's motto is taken from right out of Thoreau's *Walden:* "Simplify, simplify." Although admittedly only a "mediocre" programmer himself, Kapor inspired former Data General software engineer Jonathan Sachs to simplify and keep simplifying the program. "Kapor has strong user empathy," lauded *Fortune,* "a rare mind-set among the technical virtuosos of high tech. He can sit in front of a half-finished program and weed out routines that seem obvious to the technically literate, but would bewilder ordinary users." Because of his customer empathy, Kapor took pains to make his instruction manual easy to understand. To help users learn Lotus, he created tutorial discs to accompany the program.

Equally important, Kapor borrowed ideas from outside the computer industry to market Lotus. When he launched 1-2-3, he bought splashy full-page ads in *Newsweek, Time,* the

Wall Street Journal, and other publications rather than just in computer magazines, because he wanted to reach business-people.

To Don Burr and Mitch Kapor, coming up with entirely new ideas wasn't required. What both did was to combine existing ideas in a novel way that better served their customer group. These ideas came from within and outside their own fields.

To a great extent innovation is *knowing which ideas to borrow.* This realization can make you more observant of ideas you might borrow to build a Breakthrough Idea. In addition, this realization reminds us that innovators are made, not born. Kapor was a "perpetual graduate student" who never graduated, as well as a former disc jockey and stand-up comic who had an interest in computers. As *Esquire's* Frank Rose pointed out, few people took Kapor seriously when he announced he was going to set up a software firm. One Harvard Business School instructor who knew Kapor at the time confessed, "I thought it was a good idea—I just didn't think he could do it."

The same principle of borrowing and combining ideas is at work outside the business arena. Marva Collins' teaching methods were not new. Her success as an educator came from combining traditional, supposedly outdated ideas, such as the phonics method of pronunciation and spelling, with new ideas where the old ones weren't working. Collins also dared to challenge the impersonal, testing-oriented teaching style with one that emphasized character building and morality. She instilled her belief that even ghetto children could break out of the environment through hard work and study.

You too can borrow and combine ideas from within and outside of your field. Focus on how your Breakthrough Idea can best serve the intended customer group. You will be surprised at the results.

179

Step 4: Obtain Feedback

Because innovators are constantly generating and implementing ideas, they develop a sixth sense.

It springs from an orientation to feedback and from a belief that answers exist if we are willing to search for them. It is developed daily in testing out smaller ideas and in analyzing failures. It doesn't matter how much quantitative data is available. Innovators seek feedback no matter how many people are involved in deciding whether or not to launch an idea.

Innovators have different names for obtaining feedback. One calls it "my own market research system." Another calls it his "due diligence" process. No two styles of obtaining feedback are the same. Some people prefer to try their ideas out on a lot of people and encourage them to shoot down their ideas. They are extremely comfortable with people tearing up anything they suggest. Uncomfortable with argumentative give-and-take, others prefer to seek feedback indirectly, asking questions that don't indicate why they are being asked. As one innovator described it, "I know people with touchy egos who still manage to test their ideas out and keep the probability of success pretty high."

> *Attention to feedback is a critical reason innovators succeed. Feedback acts as a "checks and balances" system to keep you from overlooking weaknesses or better alternatives.*

Doug Greene, chairman of New Hope Communications, bounces any potential Breakthrough Idea off ten to fifteen people. However, this doesn't mean he always does what the feedback suggests. When he asked people what they thought of the word *delicious* for a new magazine, all of them said they didn't like the name.

"Whenever I ask anybody for feedback, I prepare myself to realize that people are giving me their best opinion," Greene told us. "But you have to realize that no matter who they are, they may not know either." Greene is not taking a poll when he seeks feedback. He wants to see how what others say makes him feel about his idea. And he's also looking for fresh input, new angles to consider, new things to think about. Experience tells him that he is bound to receive some knee-jerk reactions. "I find a lot of my really powerful ideas scare people," he says. "When people get afraid, they'll always say no."

When ten people told Greene that *Delicious!* wasn't a good concept, his initial euphoria turned to caution. He said to himself, "I really like this idea, but something isn't right about it. Let me just say good-bye to it and it will come back if it's important." Seven months later it was back in his mind again. He began noticing the word everywhere. He says: "If you feel strongly about something after hearing ten no's, odds are you've got something really good." Today, Greene calls *Delicious!* "one of our most incredible successes."

Most of us have witnessed someone trying to make an idea work who let it be known that he or she didn't want to hear what anybody had to say about it. Perhaps you've taken this attitude yourself. We become so excited about our idea's potential that we forget to test it out on others, to enlist their help in finding its weaknesses and discovering its strengths.

Innovators, by contrast, don't wince when you criticize their ideas. They may not like what you have to say, but they know they need to discover flaws *now* rather than after they've begun the launch. So important is this process that innovators have developed techniques for obtaining honest feedback.

Five Tested Ways to Obtain Feedback

Obtaining feedback sounds easy. In reality, few of us know *how* to ask for it. Most people don't really want honest opinions, for when they ask for "feedback," they really want approval.

How to obtain feedback on your idea? Become feedback-oriented! Go to your network of friends and associates. Make appointments with people knowledgeable in the area you're attempting to innovate within. Seek out anyone and everyone you think can help you build the idea. While it's best not to expose your idea to negative persons, keep in mind that almost everyone you talk to about your idea will give you something of value.

A. Write out your idea in detail. The act of writing it down will help you clarify your thinking. State your assumptions. List the questions you must answer. For example, Bill Reed might have written: "I believe that after hearing my speech on reading, parents will be motivated to buy fifty dollars' worth of books." Or: "I believe that if I send out one thousand mailers, I can expect three percent of the people to show up at my seminar." Then type it up.

B. Try your idea out on your spouse or close friend first. By articulating your idea, you are apt to discover its flaws. Most of the innovators we interviewed cited their spouses as their initial sounding boards. The second most-often mentioned source was the innovator's business partner.

C. Solicit feedback from outside experts. Don't rush to set up appointments with experts. Their time is valuable and the way to enlist their support is to impress them with the thoroughness of your preparation. They will take you more seriously (and work harder to help you) if you are prepared.

Save the smartest people you can find for last. By then, you will have ironed out the obvious bugs and they can help you look at the major issues.

D. Show people you mean business. Schedule an appointment at a time convenient to them, when their thinking is fresh and their minds are clear. Write out a list of questions you want to ask beforehand. Focus on what you most want from that person. Maintain control of the meeting with your questions.

E. Don't try to evaluate the helpfulness of the feedback while you're receiving it. When you are obtaining feedback from someone, you are really asking him or her to do some creative thinking on your behalf. The two of you are essentially brainstorming together. Encourage the other person to risk thinking out loud. Play devil's advocate with the advisor. Later you can determine the value of that feedback.

Remember the four steps of building an idea: Avoid Premature Closure; Gather Strategic Information; Borrow and Combine Ideas; Obtain Feedback. These four steps can help you avoid the kind of mistakes that plagued Bill Reed and his attempt to get a reading seminar off the ground. But rather than dwell on an example of failure, let's now turn to someone who successfully incorporated the four steps to launch an idea.

How Bill Thompson Built His Breakthrough Idea

While the problems of American agriculture are now obvious to everyone, they became obvious to Bill Thompson a decade ago. Thompson is chairman of California-based Thompson Vitamins (founded by his father in 1935) and the owner of a thousand-acre cattle ranch in Vienna, Missouri.

In the early 1970s, Thompson found cattle ranching a difficult business. What profit he generated went to the bank for interest payments. As a result, he sold off his herd, paid off the ranch's debts, and was thinking about selling out when it occurred to him that he was giving up without knowing what he was doing wrong. His was one of the better-managed ranches in the state. Why had ranching become such a high-risk business? Was there an alternative?

In the 1970s, American agriculture had become dependent on energy, chemicals, and expensive farm equipment. Thompson noticed that many farmers had become detached from the land and had lost touch with local markets. Growers and consumers were often thousands of miles apart, necessitating transportation which added to the cost of food but did not benefit the farmer. "I realized," Thompson told us, "that American farming was in so much trouble structurally that it was going to change. The minute you recognize that we are investing twenty kilocalories of fossil fuel for every calorie of food we're producing, you know there's going to be a change. It's only a question of *when*."

Thompson decided he wanted to be part of that change. He began to see that the persons who solved these growing problems could create a significant opportunity for themselves. The more he read and talked to other farmers and farm economists, the more determined he was to find a solution. Conventional agriculture, he could see, suffered from a thinking rut that said, in effect: "There is no way but the present way to grow food profitably. Alternative methods, such as 'organic farming,' have already been tried and they just don't work." Thompson agreed that both methods had inherent problems: "On the one hand you go broke; on the other hand your yields per acre go down." But to Thompson, organic farming was not the only alternative. He believed there had to be a third alternative, and he was determined to find it.

184

The search became an obsession. Over the next five years, Thompson read every book, journal, and article about agriculture he could get his hands on. He did not look at this as work, but as fun, something to challenge him as he continued to expand his vitamin business. Devoid of the prejudices so much a part of present-day agribusiness, he read what the "conventional" farming advocates were saying, and he read what the "organic" people were saying. He networked with everybody, talking to hundreds of farmers and farm economists all over the United States.

Thompson wasn't just looking at the problems of farmers. His unconventional thinking led him to challenge conventional assumptions about the kind of food consumers wanted. Since he was working for their benefit, he studied consumers' changing values and priorities. Here his experience in the natural-foods business was helpful. As his vitamin business grew steadily each year, he clearly recognized that he was riding the health-and-fitness Wave that took hold during the 1970s. His accumulated observations told him that there was a growing minority of consumers who wanted food that looked and tasted good and had a high level of nutrition. What they didn't want was pesticide residues. If given a choice, they would opt for organically grown fruits and vegetables from local sources.

Discovery, it is said, comes to the prepared mind. After five years of part-time research and thinking, Bill Thompson had a Breakthrough Idea. On Labor Day, 1978, he wrote in a notebook a twenty-page description of his idea, which he believed was the third alternative he had been looking for.

Like many innovations, the idea contained very little that was new. It was a combination of two existing but little-known methods. The first is called French Intensive Bio-Dynamic gardening, which advocates growing a number of crops together in tight bunches rather than in rows. The second method Thompson describes as "a kind of overarching philosophical approach to the plant world first articulated by the visionary German philosopher Rudolf Steiner."

Bio-Dynamic gardening was pioneered by the British horticulturist Alan Chadwick, who had practiced his techniques on a gardening scale. Thompson believed that the method could be adapted to farming, both to diminish the need for pesticides and herbicides and to attain high yields per acre of the highest-quality food, even under adverse climatic conditions. With its focus on crop diversity as opposed to monoculture (the growing of a single crop), Bio-Dynamic farming also lent itself to local marketing of fresh food.

The idea was sparked when Thompson challenged several basic assumptions of conventional agriculture. Among these were the assumptions that bigger was better and that monoculture, or single-crop farming, was the only way to survive. Thompson had come to believe that monocropping created many of the conditions that required the use of pesticides, heavy and expensive farm equipment, irrigation, and other problems. "If you shifted away from monoculture," he explained, "many of those problems ceased to exist. Instead of trying to throw more and more money at trying to make the old approach more effective, we completely changed the approach."

There were scores of questions Thompson needed to answer before he would know whether the idea was feasible. The first one: Had anyone already tried the idea at the farm level? If so, he didn't want to reinvent the wheel. But in checking around, he realized he would have to start from scratch.

To network for Strategic Information, Thompson formed a nonprofit organization called the American Farm Foundation.

He persuaded prominent individuals to become members of its board of directors, including Robert Bergland, former secretary of agriculture, and Dan Ritchie, chairman of Westinghouse Broadcasting. Since a major goal was to reduce purchased inputs of energy, Thompson delved into a study of alternative energy sources. He retained a solar power expert on his board of advisors. He also enlisted the assistance of agriculture economist Brice Ratchford. He hired a computer specialist to advise him on the use of computers in farm management and communications. "It was a step-by-step process," Thompson explained. "I looked at an area and I'd say, 'What do I need to know in order to do this? What don't I know that I need to know? Let's find somebody to help describe the terrain and show us who the players are in those areas we don't know about.' "

As Thompson sought feedback on his idea, he encountered prejudices at every turn. "There's no market for that kind of product," many said. "It's impossible to use tractors if you plant the crops so close together." When told that he didn't intend to use tractors to cultivate the land, they said he'd never be able to afford the human labor. "It was amazing how many people, including all the recognized experts, told me it sounded wonderful but it wasn't going to work," Thompson recalled. "But it was never the same reason." And if all the experts had voiced the same objection to his idea, would he have scrapped it? "They would have had to show me *why* they didn't think it would work. The fact that they didn't think it would work wasn't enough all by itself."

Told he was crazy, Thompson pressed ahead anyhow. The more he gathered Strategic Information, sought feedback, and continued to build his idea, the more certain he became that he was onto something big. As the idea evolved, Thompson realized that it was ripe for replication. He began to see Gasconade Farm as a national concept of growing premium fruits and vegetables for local markets. As limited partnerships, they would cooperate on marketing, sales, distribution, and research. Apprentices would train at the "mother farm" in Missouri and would be responsible for recruiting investors to back them until they began operating at a profit. This way he could build his market niche much faster, and more people would be involved.

By 1982, Thompson was ready to take the next step: Launch the idea, using three hundred acres of his Missouri cattle ranch as a prototype in which to work out all the bugs in the new approach. Having learned everything he could in theory, he knew he had to literally move to the field. But before he could do this, he needed somebody to help implement the idea. He searched high and low for someone who was familiar with Alan Chadwick's horticultural methods. He found just such a person in Alan York, then co-director of the Waldorf Institute Garden in Southfield, Michigan. He and York spent hours together getting to know each other and exchanging ideas. Finally, Thompson invited York to Missouri to look at his land. After describing his vision of what it could become, he persuaded York to sign on.

Since our story is about innovation and not farming, we'll skip a few details here and summarize Gasconade Farm's remarkable progress to date. By early 1986, Gasconade was out of the research-and-development stage and into full commercial production. In fact, the company could not keep up with the demand for its quality fruits and vegetables, which now garner premium prices at St. Louis' top restaurants. Expecting to show a profit by 1989, Thompson says, "We're right on schedule."

A Final Thought About Building Your Ideas

Nolan Bushnell is right: Everyone who's ever taken a shower *has* had an idea. But it's the person who does something with that idea who makes a difference. No prelaunch procedure can ever guarantee that an idea will be a winner. But by gathering Strategic Information, soliciting feedback, and looking for ideas to borrow, you increase the chances your idea will succeed.

Once an innovator has gestated an idea, he or she is ready to take the plunge and attempt to implement it. Here's where many people get cold feet. But not innovators. They have developed aptitudes and skills in taking risks. We'll learn about those special skills in the next chapter.

TEN

The Elements of Risk Taking

One man with courage makes a majority.

Andrew Jackson

In the years after the Great Depression, America embarked upon an attempt to eradicate risk. We asked the government to guarantee our savings. We bought billions of dollars worth of insurance. We sought lifetime employment with guaranteed cost-of-living increases each year to protect us from inflation. Executives awarded themselves generous "golden parachutes"

190

in case they came out on the losing end of a merger or take-over.

This national experiment had many obvious benefits. But it also had a less obvious down side. As risk avoidance became a fixation, we forgot that risk can also be a positive force. We forgot that progress occurs when people take chances. And instead of finding security, we discovered boredom, mediocrity, and lack of opportunity.

Today more and more people realize that risk can bring about rewards. The national mind-set is shifting. Those who would have entered "safe" careers a generation ago now enter arenas that require and encourage risk taking. Suddenly, risk takers are new heroes.

Yet what does it mean to be a risk taker? Viewed through the lens of the media, it is easy to start believing that risk takers are innately different from the rest of us. They emerge larger than life from the magazine profiles and television interviews. But if we allow ourselves to believe that risk takers are somehow different, we give ourselves an excuse not to act. "I've got friends who have absolutely brilliant ideas for new businesses," one innovator told us. "They spend months and months saying, 'I'm going to do this,' and 'I'm going to do that.' But they don't go through with it."

Even those who venture to dip a toe in the pond of risk never allow themselves to get used to the water, as psychiatrist David Viscott observes in his book *Risking:*

> It is surprising how little most people know about taking risks. Often they become inhibited by fear at the very moment they must commit themselves to action. At the first sign of a reversal they hesitate and, fearing that the situation is about to fall apart, retreat untested, convinced that they were in over their heads, thankful just to escape.

Viscott is right—most of us have never become comfortable with risk. Yet to survive and succeed in the Innovation Age, you must take prudent chances. To do this, it is necessary to develop a healthy attitude toward risk taking.

How to Turn Risk Into a Positive Force

Risk avoidance does not allow you to solve problems or create opportunities. Putting yourself at risk means staking something valuable to create the life you want.

Innovators have a unique approach to risk taking. They are hardly the gamblers that the media portrays. Few of them we encountered appeared to enjoy making deals in which the deal was the end rather than the means. Innovators don't get a thrill out of taking risks; they get a thrill out of implementing their ideas. They know that risk is necessary when you are doing something that has never been done before. Although they may "bet the store," they do so out of the belief that their idea will ultimately prevail.

This type of risk taking is growth-oriented. Growth, rather than money, is the highest reward. It requires us to stretch our competencies to their utmost and then to go beyond. And it is exhilarating, as magazine publisher and entrepreneur Doug Greene can attest:

> When you're at risk, energy flows through you that doesn't flow through you when you're not at risk. I have found that different people have different requirements for risk. I know if I don't have a tremendous amount of risk flowing through me, my machine doesn't work.

Greene and other innovators believe that taking chances makes you a more capable, self-empowered person. You figure out a way to transcend obstacles. You pay closer attention.

192

You seize opportunities. "By exposing yourself to risk," comments Gifford Pinchot, the "intrapreneuring" consultant, "you're exposing yourself to heavy-duty learning, which gets you on all levels. It becomes a very emotional experience as well as an intellectual experience. Each time you make a mistake, you're learning from the school of hard knocks, which is the best education available."

But growth is not the only reason for taking risks. Risk introduces change. Donald Freeberg is a major Southern California developer who began his career as an IBM typewriter salesman in the early 1950s. He built apartments just as the need for apartments was taking off, retirement hotels just as the need for retirement hotels was taking off, and roadside motels just as the need for motels was growing. He comments:

> Those of us who have run companies like to have our people act entrepreneurially. But I think there's a difference between being entrepreneurial within a corporation and being an entrepreneur who is out there worrying about the payroll and selling this and that to keep going. That's a different sort of thing. Sleepless nights? Sure. And particularly if you've got somebody else's money involved with your own. When you're just starting out on something, if you've got somebody else's money it's always a friend's. It isn't like some nameless stockholder. Sure [the corporate person] can take risks; the boss expects him to fail once in a while. He's not going to stop eating if he fails. So there's a different motivation behind it and I don't think some of the management gurus recognize that.

Why One Innovator Gambled It All . . . and Won Big

As vice-president of software development at Data General, Bill Foster had an enviable position. In his early thirties, Foster was already pulling in one hundred thousand dollars a year.

193

In a few more years his unvested stock options would be worth a million dollars. Yet in July 1979, he left behind the stock options and the cushy job to take a very big risk.

"I'd been hemming and hawing about quitting for a couple of years," Foster told us. His desire to start a business began in 1978. On a family vacation to the Bahamas, Foster took along a notebook, planning to spend the week working up some ideas. He returned with a tan and a blank notebook. "I got home and said to myself, 'Ah, you're too old. Just forget it . . . just be happy doing what you're doing.' "

He thought he had shoved the idea out of his mind. Then, while in London on business a year later, the idea suddenly recurred—at two in the morning. "You're going to do it this time. You're going to quit your job and start a company." Foster pulled out his notebook and started writing down ideas. He started to formulate a business plan. He started thinking about where he could get money. The next morning he called his wife and said, "Honey, when I get back, I'm going to quit." She said, "Yeah, sure you are."

Two weeks later Foster was no longer an employee of Data General. His former colleagues thought he was crazy. A friend took him out sailing to tell him many people were convinced he'd been fired. They couldn't believe he would quit.

Foster left because trying to build his own company while still working for Data General would have been "unethical and horribly complicated." So he quit when parts of his Breakthrough Idea were still unresolved. He had only the barest outline of an idea. He had a year's salary saved up. But he had a dream.

His idea was straightforward, ambitious: to compete head-on with Tandem Computers, a Silicon Valley manufacturer of "fault tolerant" equipment, which is guaranteed not to lose data even during power outages. Tandem's innovative founders had correctly anticipated the growing need for such computers and the difficulty of major computer companies in entering this market. As a result, Tandem had this sizable niche all to itself.

Foster wanted to do something more than produce a copycat product. This was something David Packard, one of the cofounders of Hewlett-Packard, had drummed into his engineers. "Make a technical contribution," Packard implored. "Innovate; don't emulate." *But how could he do it better?*

Tandem's computers used software as the basis of their failsafe system. When Tandem was founded, this made a great deal of economic sense; hardware was expensive relative to software. But since then, the cost of hardware had plummeted, while the cost of software had steadily increased. Foster remembers, "I finally realized that the cost of hardware was so cheap that this was the best way to go. It wasn't that I looked at the cost first and said, 'Let's do it that way.' I said, 'Let's do it that way, now what's wrong with that?' And cost turned out to be a favorable factor."

Now all he had to do was sell the idea. "I started with the assumption that I could sell myself and this idea so well that people would invest in me," he said. "I was never a really great engineer, but I was always pretty comfortable selling my ideas. The problem was, I had no knowledge of venture capital at all. I just kind of naively presumed that there was a lot of money out there and that someone would invest in me. It took me a while to figure out that that was totally wrong. I was extremely confident when I left Data General, and then things went steadily downhill from there."

By Christmas 1979, Foster didn't want to attend any parties. "I didn't want to see all these people who were still working, who still had money coming in. For the first time in my life I was withdrawing money from my savings every week. It was a strange feeling. Having been conditioned to save and put money away, I never realized how I would react to taking it out. It was a very depressing thing to do. I actually started to believe some of the people who told me I had made a big mistake."

Fighting off doubts, Foster worked furiously. He worked "almost every waking moment" with an energy and conviction he had never experienced before. He continued gathering Strategic Information, seeking out feedback, and building his idea. Much of his time was spent seeking venture capital. "I made millions of phone calls. I learned to follow up on every lead, to talk to everyone who would talk. If someone suggested I call someone, I'd call him. I would read about someone in *Venture* or *Inc.* magazine who started a company and I'd call him up and go visit him. The thing that really amazed me was how much everyone liked to talk about what they had done and how they had done it. I'd ask them what the problems were and they would spill everything. I'd ask for a copy of their business plan and was surprised how willing they were to share it with me. The reason I wanted to see their business plan was because I was trying to figure out how to format mine."

Desperate for funding, Foster arranged an appointment with a bank. When he arrived, he was informed that his appointment had been canceled. Disgusted, he stopped by to visit Robert Freiburghouse, who owned a small software company nearby. Toward the end of their conversation, Foster gave Freiburghouse the copy of his business plan he had brought along for the bank appointment. "He called me that evening," Foster said. "He told me, 'This is better than what I'm doing. How would you like to have a partner?' "

From here on out, Foster's Breakthrough Idea began to fly. Freiburghouse came on board to take charge of software development. Venture capital began to flow. In May 1980, Stratus opened for business. Twenty-one months later, the first product was shipped. Sales of its computers reached $5.5 million in 1982, $20.6 million in 1983, $42 million in 1984, and $80 million by 1985.

Bill Foster on Taking Risks

What does Foster see as his most important attribute that allowed him to take such a risk? "Not being afraid of failing," he says without hesitation. "When I think about why in the past I didn't go off and try to do something like this, it was more fear of failure than not thinking I could succeed. I guess finally I woke up to the fact that it didn't matter if I failed—that was the worst reason in the world not to try. I certainly don't consider myself a special person. When I was a kid I was an underachiever; no one really had very big expectations for me. I consider myself a very normal person. I'm not smarter than other people. I don't have any clever ideas. But when you say, 'Why don't people act on their dreams?' my answer is that most people don't like to take chances."

Do you have to take risks to succeed? Foster thinks so, but adds:

> What I've found is that when you analyze the risks, they're probably not as great as you think. The risk is more of an ego risk. It's a matter of whether or not your ego can accept failure. But there's no question that you have to take some gambles if you're going to innovate and succeed.

Perhaps most importantly, Foster had role models of other innovators around him. This was important to him because he

197

was able to realize that they weren't really any different. "I drew the conclusion that they didn't walk on water," he explained, "so I decided if they could do it, I could at least try. It was worth the risk."

The Role of Timing in Assessing Risk

Buckminster Fuller once claimed to have determined the lag time between inventions and their coming into use to be twenty-two years, and fifty years in the home-building industry in which he was most involved.

If only it were so predictable. Then all an innovator would have to do is create a new product or service or method and wait twenty-two years for its introduction. Unfortunately, it's not that simple. When you're about to take a risk you must confront a number of questions: How will the intended customer group respond to your idea? How much time and energy and struggle will be required to turn your vision into reality?

Innovators are not interested in having their ideas pay off after they are gone. Timing, therefore, becomes a critical issue in determining risk. Innovators want others to use and benefit from their idea in the foreseeable future. That payoff can come soon or it can come about over a period of years. Bill Thompson, for example, was willing to devote sixteen years to building his network farm concept.

But can you really say when an idea will pay off? In our study of America's leading innovators, we found little agreement as to how to assess timing, or even what ratio of luck to skill is involved. Bill Foster, for example, believes luck played a "fair sized" role. "I know everyone says you make your own luck, but if I'd left in 1977, I'm convinced that the money wouldn't have been there. It turned out that in 1979 and 1980 venture capital was just starting to open up again because of the reduction of the long-term capital-gains tax, which became law in 1978."

Management author Tom Peters would agree with Foster. He believes timing is largely a matter of luck. He uses *In Search of Excellence* as an example. "Had Bob Waterman and I written exactly the same book, with every semicolon in place, five years earlier," he says, "nobody would have bought it because the world wasn't ready for it. We translated a set of ideas at exactly the time that the demand was there. We were lucky that what we were doing happened to match the needs of the time." In other words, Peters doesn't think that innovation can ever become a systematic process:

> I don't think you can plan that you are going to be the person who is the translator of an idea. I think there are three thousand things in my career background, personal background, plus Bob Waterman's background, times the context, times the exact timing of the Japanese, and so on, that intersected to make us the right people for the right time to have done what we did. The mix is so subtle that for you to decide that you are going to pull these things together and make these connections occur is silly. Maybe you will do it and maybe you will see yourself that way, but the reality of it is you were lucky, because you were the right person at the right time.

To Peters, Steve Jobs and Steve Wozniak, founders of Apple Computer, were "very practical people who happened to stumble across an incredible opportunity that they were in a position to exploit. Had they been born ten years before, they would have happily done their thing at the Home Brew Club [an early San Francisco Bay Area computer club] and never gotten beyond the Heathkit stage." And had Fred Smith come along five years earlier or five years later, Peters sees no reason to believe he would have amounted to anything more than "one more small businessman, a successful entrepreneur, perhaps."

Fred Smith did not disagree with Peters. "The idea that made up Federal Express absolutely would not have worked five years previously for many, many reasons, and five years later the market that was emerging which led to the realization that there was a need for Federal Express would have been served one way or another." But having said that, Smith went on to say that he thinks existing companies *can* be more systematic in timing their innovations because they have more resources. He pointed to IBM's momentous decision to "bet the company" and build the 360 series computer ("it was the difference between IBM being the fabulous, perhaps the greatest, company of all time and an IBM that would resemble today's National Cash Register"), to Bill Allen's decision at Boeing to build the 747, and Al Neuharth's decision at Gannett to start *USA Today.*

Another point of view about timing is represented by those who think innovation is a matter of skill. This camp believes it is up to the innovator to find the needs that aren't being met. Most important, it is necessary to *sell the customer group on the idea.* The presumption is that customers don't really know what they want until they see it.

Video pioneer Stuart Karl looks at timing this way:

> I never think about timing. I'm always late, that's the way I look at it. By the time I'm getting it [an idea], it already should have been done. So maybe that's why I'm early, because I'm always thinking I'm late. I remember very well when there was no *Jane Fonda's Workout* video and there was a shortage of funds. And I just said to people, "Don't worry about it, we'll get there." It's like the guy who

works at it all hours of the night and day. He's going to have more luck making it work out because he's flexible. I'm flexible. I move. I solve. I always tell people who sit around and worry about this and how you can't do that that they're going to fail. *You have to go for it.*

The issue here is whether the innovator creates the Wave, or whether the Wave creates the innovator. The Wave is, of course, but a metaphor for an amalgamation of forces and shaping factors. Now that we have a Federal Express, does this create the need for overnight delivery by extending the absolute deadline of Jones in Seattle, who is preparing the report for Smithers in Denver? Did *In Search of Excellence* create the excellence movement in America by showing us that we did not have to look to Japan for role models of well-run companies? Did Marva Collins become a nationally celebrated teacher because the nation was looking for educational excellence in its inner cities? Did *Jane Fonda's Workout* video create the exercise craze or did the exercise craze create Jane Fonda? People like Stuart Karl believe the innovator creates the trend, although the innovator, via his or her skills, is able to seize the opportunity. And no matter what position one takes on this issue, all innovators would agree that, as Karl says, you have to go for it.

Are You Ready to Take the Heat?

These days we no longer hang people for proposing new ideas, burn them at the stake, or force them to drink hemlock. But innovators must still withstand some heat. You must deal with the weight of the past and resistance to change. When you introduce improvements or new ideas, you upset the status quo. This causes fear in those whose minds are set in the Sustainer Mode.

Sometimes that fear comes from others in your profession. This happened to John Shea. After graduating from Harvard Medical School and fighting in the Korean War, Shea went to Europe to, as he puts it, "complete my education myself." While there he came upon a problem that he very much wanted to solve: otosclerosis, a form of arthritis that attacks the sound-conducting bones of the middle ear. Working eighteen-hour days, he read through volume after volume of yellowed medical journals, researching the problem. In the basement autopsy room of Vienna Hospital, he dissected the ears of hundreds of cadavers.

Then one blizzardy Sunday evening, as Shea sat reading in his overcoat in the unheated Vienna University Library, the solution occurred to him. It was a procedure called the stapedectomy, which had been briefly tried in the early 1900s and then abandoned as ineffective. Shea thought he knew why the operation worked only part of the time. In patients with otosclerosis, the tiny stapes bone becomes frozen in place, unable to vibrate and conduct sound. Stapedectomy, as it had been practiced, simply removed the stapes bone. Sometimes the eardrum grew in such a way that it was able to conduct sound, but often it didn't. In a flash it became obvious to him that the solution was to recreate the sound-conducting mechanism, not by dropping the eardrum but by creating an artificial stapes.

Shea headed back to the United States to see if his solution worked. He experimented with dozens of materials and finally developed one made of Teflon. In May 1956, he performed his first successful stapedectomy. Then he faced the heat of his profession.

The scene was an international medical conference of ear surgeons, where the thirty-one-year-old doctor went to present his findings. Just before he was to speak, he was pulled aside by a friend of his late father. "Don't do it, John," the doctor warned. "If you go out there and present these cases, you're going to disgrace yourself and your father and ruin your reputation forever. You'll never amount to anything. I beg you not to make this presentation."

"There I was," Shea reflected, "trying to get started and to be respectful to this older man and he was telling me not to do what I had worked so hard on. Finally I just said, 'Look, I'm sorry. I wish I could accommodate you, but I know I'm right. I've done these operations and I owe it to these people and to myself. I have to tell about it.' "

Shea made his presentation that day, and the reception he received was predictable. For the next two years, he was ostracized. Some of his colleagues saw the light, but most rejected his solution out of hand. To them, stapedectomy was an idea whose time had come and gone. And they didn't want it to come back again.

Today, Shea is philosophical when he talks about facing the heat. "The people who oppose you the most," he says, "are those who represent the establishment your innovation will overthrow. And the people who criticized what I had done were the people doing another operation, called a fenestration, which created a window in another part of the ear. This operation was difficult to do and gave only fair results, and only a small number of surgeons could do it well. The stapedectomy threatened them. At first their pride was involved because here was somebody coming along and making them look silly. And of course they were making a lot of money from it."

John Shea faced the heat within his profession. But some innovators have to face it within the organization they work for. Tom Peters, for example.

How Tom Peters Faced the Heat

The perception many people have of Tom Peters, coauthor with Robert Waterman of *In Search of Excellence,* is that he didn't have to face any heat in bringing forth his ideas. The story Peters tells is quite different:

> I encountered huge amounts of prejudice. To get to where we were in 1980 when we started the book was a struggle every day. The project I was working on started in 1976. And from about the second day of that project until the day I left McKinsey [the international consulting firm where Peters and Robert Waterman worked, and which sponsored their research], it was multiple battles every day. I was essentially fired from McKinsey in 1981, so there was an effort at personal discrediting that matched the discrediting of the ideas. The interesting thing is that they discredit the person rather than the ideas. Then, after the ideas become a success, the next step is to say that there's nothing new in them. Every innovator will find both forms of prejudice because if people are threatened by the idea, they will find a way to invalidate you personally, which is a lot easier than invalidating your ideas.

How Economist Arthur Laffer Faced the Heat

In a restaurant in Washington in 1974, Arthur Laffer and an official of Gerald Ford's administration were excitedly talking about whether or not the president should propose a tax increase. Laffer urged a tax cut instead, arguing that his research convinced him that the less government taxed, the more revenues it would take in. On a cocktail napkin, Laffer sketched a curve that showed his concept clearly and simply. Although Ford never submitted the tax increase, Laffer's Curve took on a notoriety all its own. In 1978, Californians passed Proposition

13, setting off a nationwide tax revolt. Laffer's Curve was often cited as a justification. It was then that Laffer's ideas came to the attention of candidate Ronald Reagan, who became one of Laffer's biggest supporters.

Today, Laffer is known as the intellectual godfather of the tax-cut movement. But in the halls of academia, Laffer's unconventional ideas have been met with much less enthusiasm. Like many innovators, Laffer did not invent or create many of the ideas for which he is best known. Laffer gives economist Robert Mundell credit for "discovering" supply-side economics. Laffer first came upon Mundell's ideas while earning his Ph.D. at Stanford in the mid-sixties. He then went to Chicago for a faculty appointment under Mundell. But in expanding upon Mundell's ideas with his own, Laffer became the point man for selling the supply-side theory to a customer group, in this case the general public.

"Once you're on that path of discovery," he told us, "you can't get off. The only way you can get off is if you become insecure and you decide to go in a corner and sit there and stop yourself." Mundell didn't want the heat. Laffer didn't mind it. And he got plenty of it.

Leading the attack on the upstart supply-siders was Paul Samuelson, the famed economist of the Keynesian school. Laffer vividly recalls the time he first listened to a tape Samuelson recorded called, *Why They're Laughing at Laffer.* "That was a serious thing for a twenty-eight-year-old professor, let me tell you," said Laffer. "It shook the very foundations. I mean even if you believed you were right, the question then was: Would the academic world allow you to survive? Paul Samuelson has enormous power. So does the profession. And it uses its power in a collusive and persecutory fashion all the time. They really do persecute people."

Although he was promoted to tenure at Chicago, Laffer's supply-side ideas put a temporary stop to his career. For five years he was denied a raise. His articles were rejected by major academic journals. But Laffer never backed off; instead he dug deeper. The more he researched, the more it checked out.

"I was getting suffocated under this huge bolt called my profession," he said. "And I knew I could never reprove myself to get their accolades. It was obvious that I, Arthur Laffer, would never be praised by Paul Samuelson."

What gave him the confidence to continue, Laffer noted, was his family background. His father had been the president of a major corporation, and his mother had been a grand jury foreman in the 1950s. He also knew that if the heat became unbearable he could do something else. "There are three escape routes outside academics," he said. "Business, politics, and the press." Eventually he would use all three.

As innovators like Laffer realize, other people's prejudices will dog you as long as you innovate. But Laffer believes the effect is for the better:

> It's creative dynamics. If you aren't willing to fight for [your idea] to the wall, you probably won't develop it as well as you should. Just don't personalize [facing the heat]. The thing is, they're not after *you*. They're after what you represent. They're after the paradigm shift. The biggest mistake is to try to extract revenge, because after the victory is won, they could well become your best supporters. When I went back to Chicago [as a visiting Fellow in 1984], the love and the tears in the eyes of my former colleagues was wonderful to behold. People who had really wanted to see me die were now hugging and they're so proud and pleased with the way the world is moving.

Expect the heat. It may come from members of your own profession. It may come from your own company. It may come from the media. It may even come from your own family. Expect it—but don't let it stop you.

Risk Taking: Seven Tips From the Pros

You will never be completely ready to take a big risk. But remember: Nothing ventured, nothing gained.

You are bound to be criticized for innovating. If you can't stand the heat, you'll never be able to take a risk. And if you aren't able to take risks, you'll never be able to innovate. Size up the resistance. Anticipate where the heat will come from. And be flexible enough to overcome objections to your approach.

Be prepared to sell your idea to an indifferent world. Don't expect people to care about your idea. They won't, unless the idea solves their problem or creates an opportunity. They still won't, until you sell them on the benefits.

Be sure all your ducks are in order before you launch an idea. But if there are ducks that can't be put in order and you've weighed the odds and still believe the idea is doable, go for it anyway!

Challenge your assumptions about risk taking. Interview risk takers about how they approach the issue. Learn how they size up risks, how they measure the up side and the down side, and how they inform their intuition on decisions involving risk.

You don't have to take the full risk all at once. You can turn an avocation into your vocation gradually, after you have gotten all the bugs out of it. You can test market your idea on a limited basis. Take "baby steps" until you learn to walk.

Don't take a risk until you've established a firm goal. Ask yourself: What do I want to achieve by taking this risk? Is this risk really necessary? After you've satisfied yourself that you've made the right decision, launch your idea.

You don't have to assume all the risk yourself. Partners or lenders can share risk. And the people you recruit to share your dream can also. In fact, as we interviewed innovators around the country, we discovered that almost all of them were exceptionally adept at building a team. The following chapter sets out some of the team-building secrets they shared with us.

ELEVEN

Building Your Team

You can't do it alone.

Bill Gore

They met through a mutual acquaintance. He introduced himself on the telephone as Mitch Kapor and said he was starting a software company. He needed someone to help him keep things together. Was she interested? When Janet Axelrod said yes, Mitch asked to come by for a chat.

They talked for hours. They sat on the sofa in Janet's apartment and talked about where they had come from, what they believed in, and what they wanted to do with their lives. Janet told Mitch she didn't know a thing about the software business. He said it didn't matter. What they were really doing was finding out whether they liked each other and could work together.

Janet had been working as a fund raiser/organizer for the Boston Haymarket People's Fund, an association that collected money for antipoverty organizations. Now she was looking for a new challenge. And Mitch was planning to change the world.

Not that he laid a grand vision on her. "This seems like a really good idea," she remembers him saying. "Take it from me, this is where the future is." What struck her about Mitch was his understated self-confidence, the sense that he just might be able to push back the frontier of software technology.

Janet showed up for her first day of work in the living room of Mitch's apartment in Belmont, Massachusetts. Her first assignment was to find the company an office. Soon Mitch brought in two more people he knew, and the four of them took turns answering the phone. When this became a hassle they hired a receptionist. Then a Data General programmer named Jonathan Sachs joined Mitch and the two of them began working on a program they called "1-2-3."

Something significant seemed to happen every day. Whenever they needed another person, somebody would say, "I know someone we should talk to," and they would try to recruit that person. "Mitch would be vulnerable with people," Axelrod told us. " 'We have this idea,' he would say. 'We don't know if it's going to work, but we're going to give it a shot and we need you to help us.' "

The company, which became Lotus Development Corporation, did not stay small for long. In 1981, its first year, sales were $53 million. By 1985 they were $225 million, and Lotus had become the world's largest independent software company.

The Seven Essentials of a Winning Team

Throughout this book we have focused on "the person who started it all." Yet this emphasis belies an important truth about implementing innovative ideas: You can't do it alone. The fact is, you need other people to help you. You need to build a team. Even if you work "alone," as a sole proprietor, your team consists of your family, friends, colleagues, mentors, customers, advisors, and everyone else who helps you.

In recent years, much has been written about building winning teams, and for good reason. The new era demands organizational teamwork of a higher order. People are the "hard assets" of today's successful organization, not equipment, buildings, or capital. Therefore, attracting and keeping talented, creative, performance-oriented individuals is critical.

What is it about innovators that enables them to assemble a group of people and unite them in a common purpose? Surprisingly, it is not always experience. Mitch Kapor, for one, had never managed more than two or three people in his life before starting Lotus. Nor is it a particular management style. Instead, we found seven distinguishing characteristics of innovators that enable them to build winning teams:

1. the ability to communicate their vision
2. an understanding of the sources and proper uses of power
3. a desire to respond to the needs of others
4. a willingness to delegate authority
5. a tolerance for experimentation and failure
6. an ability to attract people who complement their skills
7. an ability to motivate each member of the team

Let's examine these seven characteristics more thoroughly and see how you can use them in your own team-building endeavors.

Sell Your Team on Your Vision

The vision is the *raison d'être* or "reason for being" of the team, unit, company, or organization. It is the mission, philosophy, goals, and shared values as defined by the leader and ratified by the group. It is articulated in response to such questions as: What is the purpose of this team? What are we trying to achieve?

In innovative organizations the vision is not simply to maximize profits. Innovators are primarily motivated by the challenge of turning an idea into reality. Profits are seen as a way of keeping score. Nor does it stop at "We are here to serve the needs of the customers," although the customers' needs are most important. It is more than this. At W. L. Gore and Associates, the vision is "to make money and have fun." At Federal Express, the vision is "people, service, profits." At Quality Inns, the vision is "to pursue excellence and become the most recognized, respected, and admired lodging chain in the world."

Selling and reselling the team on the vision is one of the innovator's most important responsibilities. This is no easy feat, especially for the innovator whose organization experiences hypergrowth. Here the image of the juggler trying to keep all the balls in the air is particularly appropriate. The ball that is most easily dropped is the one called "staying true to the vision." Amidst all the pressures and demands of building the organization, keeping the vision alive is not easy.

No innovator has had to face more of these pressures than

Don Burr, chairman of People Express. Burr created not only a new approach to air travel but a radically different "people" system as well. The company's growth was phenomenal. People's first scheduled flight from Newark to Buffalo took place in 1981. By 1985, People was a billion-dollar operation and the fastest-growing corporation in history.

But by mid-1986, People Express was barely afloat financially, and Burr had put the airline up for sale. Its stock price had tumbled from a high of $26 in 1983 to $5.50 a share. The company lost $58 million in the first quarter of 1986 and nearly the same amount in the second. Clearly, the bloom was off the rose; nevertheless, the airline's current troubles should not obscure the vision that gave rise to the company in the first place, fostered its breakneck growth, made millionaires out of dozens of its managers, and fundamentally changed the airline industry.

The vision underlying People Express was spelled out in a set of six precepts. The first one was service, growth, and development of people. The second was to be the best provider of airline transportation in the world, and the least expensive. The last was "to maximize profits." To accomplish this, Burr took the "no frills" concept one step further. He avoided hiring secretaries; instead, employees did their own typing. Expense accounts were prohibited, as were company cars and other perks. Anything that didn't contribute to serving the customer was not allowed.

Burr thought to eliminate bureaucracy. He didn't want "staff niches," positions that required no direct contact with customers. He wanted every manager's energies focused on the customer rather than on the bureaucracy. Even the company's chief financial officer served coffee and handled baggage. It was cross-utilization to the extreme. Burr explains:

For us it is not good enough to be commercially successful. There's something beyond that. For me it's making a better world. . . . If we end up at the end of our lifetimes having made a difference in terms of the way people see the world, in terms of the values that people share and hold and develop and work with each other on, then I think that's the thing that we would want to be remembered for most.

Burr's radical business vision required individuals who were decidedly not Organization Men and Women. They had to be caring, service-oriented, self-managed individuals who were motivated by their stake in the company. People Express used a test that screened out, as Burr put it, "antisocial, negative, cynical, downbeat characters . . . [since] that type of person isn't normally prone to be overly helpful to other people."

When the group was small and the company was new, making sure everyone understood the vision was easy. In fact, during the crazy first several years of People Express, there was a fervor among company employees. People's managers lived and breathed the business; it was their life. Burr was the guru and the message was: "Power to the employees." Harvard's D. Quinn Mills called People "the most interesting company in America" because of its "comprehensive and self-conscious effort to fit a business to the capabilities and attributes of today's work force." Reporters came around to ask questions and were infected with the spirit of cooperation and egalitarianism. They went back to their word processors and turned out glowing accounts of how teams of managers participated in decision and policymaking, of how teams of managers were elected to advisory and coordinating councils, which met with Burr and other senior managers to hammer out the company's direction.

But no honeymoon lasts forever, and even the best of preachers can exhort for only so long. While Burr was preoccupied with facilitating growth, the one-for-all vision began to wear thin. Service plummeted and less than complimentary articles began appearing in the press about unhappy customers. Several founding executives departed, reportedly after bitter disputes with Burr. As People's profitability declined, Burr allegedly became more autocratic. He also did something that was adverse to the vision; something he had previously stated he would never do: He purchased the unionized, conventionally managed Frontier Airlines, and tried to turn it into a no-frills feeder airline to give People a hub in the west. The strategy never had time to succeed. To raise much-needed cash, Burr was forced to sell Frontier to United Airlines for a fraction of what he had paid for it

Because of the media attention to him and the meteoric rise of his company, Don Burr offers an excellent example of the power of a vision to mobilize people in a common pursuit. Burr is a world-class team builder and "visionary." Because of his extraordinary ability to sell others on a vision, he was able to motivate hundreds of men and women to put forth extraordinary effort. But the complexities forced upon that team by a fast-changing, intensely competitive industry has made keeping the vision alive all the more difficult.

The point is this: The vision must be clearly defined and communicated consistently and repeatedly. Just as the United States has the Constitution and the Bill of Rights, every group that comes together to accomplish a task needs a vision. The vision inspires individuals to put the needs of the group before their own.

You Must Understand Power

When we asked Fred Smith what the most important ingredient to team building was he said, "Sublimate your own ego." "If you don't have the discipline to do that, or if you have an ego that has to be stroked all the time, then you're probably not going to be effective in building your team. Other people are just not going to respond to that."

Smith knows whereof he speaks. He readily acknowledges his ego, but he doesn't find it necessary to be the focus of attention. In fact, quite the contrary. He occasionally grants interviews and accepts speaking engagements, but only to the extent necessary to further the goals of Federal Express.

Before we were granted an interview with Smith, we were questioned carefully by a member of the corporate-communications staff who cautioned that if we intended to focus on Smith as a personality, we might as well forget it. Smith had let it be known he wasn't interested in such things. Publicity of that sort, Smith realized, is distracting to innovation.

Smith managed to make the difficult transition from founder and entrepreneur to corporate chairman. Many do not. And one problem is that their egos get in the way. Innovators must have healthy egos, otherwise they won't have the persistence and determination to continue when the heat is on. But occasionally determination becomes stubbornness.

Automaker John DeLorean, speaking about his obsession not to let "this car with my name on it go down," said that the proof he lost touch with himself was that he thought he had humility. "I was a walking disaster," DeLorean told a press conference. "Working twenty hours a day, seven days a week, taking two Seconals to get to sleep and eighteen cups of coffee to wake up," flying across the Atlantic so often, "I was walking jet lag . . . any rational human being would have taken a walk. But I was too arrogant and egotistical and did not."

One characteristic of the Baby Boom generation is that so many of them have gone to college. They have taken Psychology 101, and have read at least a few self-help books about the "games" people play. They are familiar with techniques of persuasion and manipulation, and they can talk a good line. As one Baby Boom innovator noted:

> There is a contradiction in people today. On the one hand, they realize intellectually the need for cooperation and teamwork, and that to stick to their own ideas is not always in their self-interest. But on the other hand, the child-rearing practices of the generation I grew up in were such that this is probably the most spoiled generation that has ever graced the planet. People who are spoiled are in the habit of having everything their way. So you have a contradiction going on: On the one hand you have the intellectual awareness that there is a need for cooperation, and at the same time you have this almost infantile urge. You can see it in people. You can even feel this warring in yourself at times.

There's nothing new about this warring—it is the will to power. But as Carl Jung said, "Where love reigns, there is no will to power." The innovator must be able to transcend such urges. Although we may feel this warring in ourselves, the successful team builder disciplines himself to put the needs of the team before his own.

Many of today's leading innovators take great pains to "see themselves as others see them." They avoid the trap of surrounding themselves with yes-men. The egotistical boss could survive more easily in simpler, slower times. But today, in this post-Vietnam, post-Watergate era, fewer people are willing to play in a band where the leader wants all the solos. Hardworking, creative, ambitious individuals are less willing to put up with power games.

Understand What Your Teammates Want

One reason team building has received so much attention in recent years is that the needs, expectations, and values of the 78 million members of the Baby Boom generation are now beginning to saturate the work place. They differ significantly from prior generations.

Five deep-seated characteristics are having a major impact:

1. desire for autonomy
2. desire for equality of opportunity
3. desire for meaningful work
4. desire to share in the profits
5. desire for affiliation and a sense of belonging

Robert E. Kelly, senior consultant at SRI International, examined this new generation of workers in his book *The Gold Collar Worker*. Kelly's thesis is that the Baby Boom generation has caused a revolution in the values and attitudes that shape today's work place. This new breed, says Kelly, is too intelligent to be managed by traditional methods, has little tolerance for bureaucracy, and is skeptical of authority. They expect to grow in their jobs, they respond to challenge, and they look to the work place for a sense of belonging and status.

If you haven't observed these trends in today's work force, it may be because you have not been monitoring the larger social forces. If you haven't seen these values manifesting themselves in your team, this could be a clue that you have been screening out these character types in your hiring procedures. Chances are, your organization has little new blood in it. Without realizing it, you may have established an environment where employees are not free to communicate openly, and where creativity and experimentation are stifled.

You can't afford such an environment if you want to encourage innovation. The needs of growth, challenge, belonging, and status are bound to be embodied in the talented people you need to help you implement ideas. The only effective response is to use these needs as a basis for understanding what people want, and try to meet those needs.

Remember this: The members of your team are not helping you out of the goodness of their hearts. They are working for you to get where they want to go. They may be learning new skills by working for you, and they may be exploiting the job opportunity you have created. But you'd better hope that they are not just biding their time or putting in their hours to get a paycheck. If that is their primary motivation, you're in trouble, because they aren't really team members, they're mere employees.

Give People Ownership of the Task

Of the five work place trends listed on page 218, the most important determinant of job satisfaction is work autonomy. According to a University of Michigan study, today's employees will not abide leaving their personal freedom at the doorstep. They value being able to make their own decisions and influence what happens on the job. Autonomy, according to Jeylan Mortimer, Ph.D., author of the Michigan study, is even more important to employees than the amount of pay they receive.

As a team builder, you must come to terms with this desire for autonomy. The way to attract self-actualized, creative, "can do" individuals is to demonstrate that you believe they can do their jobs without constant supervision.

Over and over again in our travels, we heard stories of tremendous accomplishments when the team leader encouraged autonomy. Robert Giaimo, the Washington restaurateur, described to us a menu change that was completed in eleven weeks, rather than the six to nine months previously required. Giaimo spent a great deal of time communicating why the change was necessary. He also encouraged a tremendous amount of planning. But he had done these same things during other menu changes. What was different this time?

> The real key was that we gave people ownership in their task. We gave them autonomy, we gave them a clear goal, we gave them complete freedom in how to accomplish it. As a result, they really signed on for it. I've learned just how important the autonomy element and ownership of the task are. We had everyone working on it—the advertising department, the marketing department, operations. Everyone had a job to do and they all had to interrelate. And because they believed in the quality of what we were doing, and because they understood the goal, it all came together. It was one of the most successful things I've ever done in my life. And we did better than when we had six to nine months to accomplish the task.

Bill McGowan, chairman of MCI, is a strong believer in autonomy. Instead of running the company from its Washington headquarters, he has divided it into seven regional divisions, which correspond to the seven former Bell companies. In each division, the leader is called president and is free to make decisions as he or she sees fit. McGowan's belief in granting autonomy was especially evident in the great long-distance telephone election concluding in September 1986. This was MCI's last big opportunity to attract customers away from rival AT&T. As a result of deregulation, telephone customers were asked to choose which long-distance carrier they wanted to handle their calls. Thereafter, gaining new customers would be much more difficult. Those wanting to switch would have to pay a fee, and the procedure would be more complicated.

Instead of running the all-important campaign from corporate headquarters in Washington, McGowan let his seven regional presidents decide on the marketing approach best suited to their areas. The seven presidents could choose to run any or none of over twenty radio and television commercials provided by headquarters. Or they could come up with their own strategies. Many did. Midwest president Ronald Spears sponsored a drive to restore Chicago's Lincoln Park Zoo and pledged one dollar to the zoo for each new subscriber. The strategy worked so well (MCI garnered about 20 percent of long-distance business there) that Spears used it in other cities in his region. MCI's Western president, Jerry Taylor, faced a different problem: a perception that AT&T was an authority figure and that upstart carriers were intruders in "Ma Bell's" territory. To counteract this image, Taylor and his team came up with the idea to include MCI ads in local phone bills. "It's an implied endorsement for us," Taylor commented.

Let People Fail

Whenever we asked innovators for their ideas on team building, one line kept coming up: "You must let people fail." Innovation is the result of experimentation, and experimentation means occasional failure.

Regis McKenna, the Silicon Valley marketing consultant, is a firm believer in the need for experimentation. His success has required that he teach subordinates his methods since he cannot possibly handle all of his company's accounts. "What you've got to do," McKenna advises, "is to not only allow but to encourage [your] people to be open and to experiment. And then you can't have any kind of retribution when they fail. You have to sit down and talk with them about it, and encourage them to keep moving. Experimentation is something that you philosophically have to believe in; it's something you have to live in everything you do."

Fred Smith adds, "You have to let people take chances and not punish them for it; they've got to have plenty of time to fail. We've been criticized about this because sometimes we've let people who failed stay in positions longer than we should have, and we've never bashed somebody in the head and run them out without dignity. We've let them fail, then even after they've failed we've tried to preserve their own sense of worth. Has that cost us? Yes, it's cost us something from the standpoint of moving with peak efficiency. But whatever it has cost us we've saved a zillion times over because people feel free to speak their minds and be innovative."

Bill Gore, chairman of W. L. Gore and Associates, says, "If you allow, encourage, and help innovations, you can count on a lot of mistakes. You have to be calm about them. You have to learn to expect them. You don't go around *trying* to make mistakes. But you do have to take risks."

Over the years, Gore and his associates (everyone at W. L. Gore and Associates is an associate) have evolved a sort of mental checklist regarding any undertaking. The list contains only two items. The first is, suppose this project, idea, or innovation turned out as successful as I could reasonably hope— would it be worthwhile? The second is, can we stand it if it's a drastic failure? If the associate answers yes to both questions, he or she may proceed—without seeking approval from anyone else in the company. If the associate judges that the failure would not be detrimental to the organization and that it is worth the risk, he can proceed without fear of reprisals if the undertaking fails. By encouraging autonomy, this system empowers every member of the team to think like a leader.

Find Teammates Who Complement Your Skills

Mo Siegel, co-founder of Celestial Seasonings Herbal Tea Company, advises, "Never hire anyone unless he's smarter than you are in the area in which he's going to be working for you."

Innovators are masters at finding the right person to get the job done. As the complexity of any undertaking increases, this becomes a critical responsibility. This is why innovators constantly network with others and observe the strengths, weaknesses, skills, and abilities of people. It is also why they seek to understand people they meet from the standpoint of, "What is this person really good at? What does this person really enjoy doing?" When they find someone they sense is good at something, they file it away. In this way they depend upon their network of contacts rather than hiring in the more traditional manner.

A superlative team cannot be assembled overnight. This is why innovators often take their teams with them wherever they go.

When Robert Hazard left IBM to become vice-president of hotels for American Express, he persuaded colleague Gerald Petitt to make the move with him. The two have worked together ever since. Hazard is the idea man, the visionary, the leader. Petitt, trained as an engineer, is the idea implementer and problem solver. Together they are a dynamic duo.

In 1974, the two left American Express to head up the Best Western lodging chain. Over the next six years they managed to increase franchise membership threefold and maneuver the

223

chain into second place in the industry, behind Holiday Inns. In 1981, after a struggling Quality Inns offered them a 20 percent equity stake to work their magic there, Hazard, Petitt, and fifteen Best Western executives accepted the offer. Ever since, Quality has been adding franchises to its system at a rate of one every other business day, making it the world's fastest-growing chain, according to the trade magazine *Hotel and Resort Industry*. It grew from 339 properties in 1981 to 900 in 1986.

"Assembling a world-class lodging team," says Hazard, "is no different from building a Super Bowl championship team. The secret is to recruit the best people, keep the group small, give everyone well-defined tasks, provide adequate funding, and then turn them loose. Their own creativity and management skills will take over and the results will be phenomenal."

Other innovators also take their teams with them wherever they go. When MIT economist David Birch formed Cognetics, Inc., an information brokerage, he brought with him four of his top graduate students. Birch, who first made a name for himself when his research shattered conventional wisdom about job creation in America, told us, "We started with a base of forty person-years under our belt. That group is a very cohesive team that has been working together for a long time. Four people don't work together for ten years lightly."

If you're thinking of leaving your company to act on an idea, consider your present colleagues for the talent you need. You already know the strengths and weaknesses of these people. Rather than starting from scratch, start with people you know.

You can't do everything, so your teammates, therefore, must compensate for your weaknesses. Many of the innovators we studied said they realized they were not "detail" persons and that they needed someone particularly good at implementing. Some examples:

Communications/entertainment entrepreneur Ted Turner has William Bevins, Jr., who the *Wall Street Journal* said "turns Ted Turner's ideas into reality."

MCI's Bill McGowan has Orville Wright. "McGowan was the visionary, the idea man, and Wright the detail man," wrote Larry Kahaner in his book *On the Line: The Men of MCI Who Took on AT&T, Risked Everything, and Won!*

In 1984, Lotus chairman Mitch Kapor promoted Jim Manzi to run the store while Kapor attends to the needs of his programmers and spends more time looking ahead to new ways to serve the users.

Aerobic Dancing pioneer Jacki Sorensen relies upon her husband, Neal, to manage the sixty-person headquarters staff of Jacki Sorensen Aerobic Dancing, Inc., in Northridge, California, and the fifteen regional managers. This allows her time to create eight new dance routines a year for twenty-five hundred instructors.

There are undoubtedly skills you lack. You may have a problem with follow-through; you may be disorganized; you may not know how to budget and manage cash flow. It's up to you to recognize *both* your strengths and your weaknesses. By admitting that you are disorganized, for example, you can then find someone who is a stickler for organization to handle that for you. Of, if you recognize that you are an idea person at heart and don't like to handle the nitty-gritty details required to implement your ideas, you can hire a "detail" person to help you.

Motivate Team Members

Traditionally, incentives were confined to the executive ranks and to pieceworkers at the very bottom of the wage scale. This is no longer true. As a result of the "three Cs," many team builders are creating new incentives for people throughout the organization. These include pay for performance plans, bonuses, employee stock ownership plans, profit sharing, and cash for good ideas.

Virtually all of the innovators we interviewed for this book had established some sort of incentive program. Ten percent of Celestial Seasonings is owned by its work force. At People Express, a third of all profits goes to the managers, and everyone is a manager. Newly hired managers are required to purchase one hundred shares of stock in the company and are provided with low-interest loans if unable to do so.

Not all incentives are monetary. The most important one turns out to be recognition, according to innovators. Giving recognition is more of an attitude than an awards program. It is not something that happens only at the end of the year; it must happen all year long. It is an *attitude*.

Other incentives involve figuring out how to give people what they want. In the "middle years" of Federal Express, for example, the company had trouble keeping its Memphis Superhub running on time. The Superhub is a cargo terminal five football fields in length and a mile around. At midnight each day of the week except Sunday, sixty-eight Boeing 727s and DC-10s descend upon Memphis from all parts of the United States, Europe, and Canada. For the next two hours several thousand employees handle each of the half million packages, sorting them via a network of conveyor belts that speed about like cars on a crowded freeway.

Hub employees are all part-timers and are primarily college students. Most attend nearby Memphis State University. Hub employees are paid nine thousand dollars a year for this fast-paced, middle-of-the-night unloading, sorting, and reloading of parcels. The great exchange must take place within two hours, otherwise the planes arrive late at their destination cities, making it necessary for couriers to rush frantically to meet the company's 10:30 A.M. delivery guarantee. The problem was, in the middle years, despite everyone's best efforts, the planes were often delayed.

In attempting to solve the problem, the company tried a number of ideas and control mechanisms, all to no avail. Finally, they realized that the reason the Hub kept running late was that it was in the best interest of employees for it to run late—it meant that they were paid overtime. The solution: Give the employees *incentives* to complete the work on time by guaranteeing them a minimum number of hours. Next, allow them to leave as soon as they got the work done. If the work was finished before the minimum hours for which they were paid, they beat the system. In a month's time, delays virtually disappeared.

What is the hallmark of a winning team? It's when everyone is motivated and creative. "Incentivizing" requires understanding the needs and desires of the individuals you lead, whether they are assembly-line workers, white-collar professionals, or a sales staff whose income is derived entirely from commissions.

In innovative organizations the methods of measuring and rewarding effort are constantly being modified and improved. If you are a team leader, you must devote time and energy to studying the arrangement by which teammates are incentivized. A paycheck is no longer enough incentive in the Innovation Age.

TWELVE

Staying On Your Game

The most dangerous moment comes with victory.

Napoleon

Y ou've done it! You've launched that Breakthrough Idea and it's working. Initial response is positive. But this is no time to let up. Because you're breaking new ground, seemingly minor mistakes and miscalculations can be disastrous if you don't catch them in time. This chapter discusses how innovators spot errors and correct them before it's too late. We call it "staying on your game."

Once you are up and running, an array of new challenges confronts you. To sustain your initial success, you must continue to innovate.

That your idea succeeded doesn't indicate *why* it did. Would-be innovators often interpret initial feedback incorrectly. Early success leads them to believe they have a Midas touch, that they've got the game figured out. Early failure causes them to retreat, convinced they "don't have what it takes." Yet the innovators in our study have had both successes and failures, and they're still winning. Let's look at how they manage to stay on their game—and how you can too.

Continue to Keep Abreast of Change

The tasks and responsibilities of implementation can, if you let them, prevent you from replicating an innovative success. After you launch an idea, reading, studying, finding dream space, exploring, networking for information, and watching trends begin to seem like luxuries. Who has time to sit quietly and read?

Innovators, that's who. They *make* the time! Focusing outward on the big picture is something they continue to do instinctively. The busier they get, the more they guard against the tendency to close off external sources of information and ideas. Nobody bats a thousand in the trend-spotting department. But sustained effort to stay on top of the wider world will pay off immeasurably.

Continue to Solicit Feedback

To ensure that your innovation stays in tune with your customers, continue to solicit feedback. This process, as we have seen, is not something innovators "devote time to." It is part of their orientation to life. It is an ongoing, conscious pattern of seeking, cross-checking, questioning, and intuitive orientation.

As Steve Jobs, former chairman of Apple Computer, discovered, playing the role of guru can distort the feedback you receive. According to Regis McKenna, Jobs "suffered from the way people deferred to him. I've told him that people were not honest with him," McKenna told *Newsweek*. [He needed people to say to him] "No, Steve, that isn't the way the world works." As a result of people deferring to his world view, Jobs didn't get the message fast enough that the market had changed from a product-led, this-is-the-latest-thing type market to a customer-driven, here's-what-we-need market. In effect, Jobs fell off his game because he wasn't tuned in to the customer group he had done so much to create.

Idolatry, as Jobs discovered, can be subversive. So can the sense of isolation that comes when no one else is doing exactly what you do. What you need are a few people with whom you can talk openly about feelings and ideas—a network of trusted advisors loyal *to you and not to the organization where you work*. Developing such trusting relationships is the best way to counteract the tendency toward mental disequilibrium in the fast-changing environments innovators inhabit.

An airplane, even though it's on autopilot, is almost constantly off course. It arrives at its destination through a series of slight but constant corrections. Feedback is your course-correction mechanism. Use it.

Continually Unhook Your Prejudices

It's the desire to prove themselves right, to show "them" that they weren't crazy after all, that drives innovators so hard to have their ideas accepted and their products, services, and methods used. Only success will vindicate them. Often, it does. But it also leaves them vulnerable to a prejudice that must be guarded against by anyone who wants to stay on his game.

Having been told they were crazy, innovators go ahead and do it anyway. And this is where the prejudice develops: Since they defied the experts once, they conclude it's best not to listen to what others say. Persistence and determination turn into stubbornness.

In his remarkable book *Innovation: The Creative Impulse in Human Progress*, British author William Kingston concludes:

> Rejection of an innovation by the men who have played a major role in the previous innovation is so common as to be almost automatic. If the earlier innovation has demanded unusual personal commitment, an individual's mind becomes so rigidly set in a particular pattern that is unable to absorb something new.

Kingston offers several classic examples. Henry Ford resisted the idea of offering consumers a wider choice of colors. ("They can have any color they want so long as it is black," he said.) Neither could Ford accept the need for the automatic starter, even after Charles Kettering had invented it and General Motors had installed it on their cars. Thomas Edison never could accept that alternating current had advantages over direct current. Albert Einstein rejected quantum physics.

What causes such prejudices to warp the innovator's thinking? Pride? Certainly. Ego? You bet. And don't forget money, as Kingston points out:

> For Edison, admitting that alternating current was more practical than his own direct current meant a loss of pride to his great rival, George Westinghouse, developer of alternating current. It also meant that Edison's plant, in which he had invested heavily, was obsolete.

It is often during periods when things are going well that prejudice arises. And then . . . the bubble bursts. Consider the

231

video game industry of the early 1980s. Lured by the chance to make megabucks, creative young computer programmers dove into game design with a passion. As Pac Man fever spread, game cartridges manufactured for $2.50 sold for $30, creating a multibillion-dollar industry overnight. America's television sets were turned into battlefields, as kids blasted away at space creatures and monsters in a blaze of colors. The programmers, many of whom were in their teens, twenties, or early thirties, were hailed as the Walt Disneys of the new era. For a while they were idolized like rock stars. But though they were raking in hundreds of thousands (sometimes millions) of dollars, featured on television programs, and hounded for autographs, they failed to challenge one assumption: that the fad would last forever.

It didn't. Almost as quickly as Pac Man fever had spread, it sputtered. The kids began to yawn. MTV was the new thing on the tube. Throwing in more bells and whistles failed to revive the fad. "We thought it could go on forever," said one disgruntled programmer who invested his profits poorly and was hit with heavy losses. "When you get the big money for the first time, you think it's never going to end." Said another, "We didn't know it was unusual to sell a million cartridges. We never really had anything to compare it to. I think we didn't realize there was a real world out there."

Keeping Your Idea Up-to-Date

Staying on your game is sometimes a matter of admitting that a competitor has come up with a better idea, and acting accordingly. This is what Jacki Sorensen, originator of Aerobic Dancing, did in response to Jane Fonda.

Sorensen, as we noted earlier, spent years introducing Aerobic Dancing to America. To her it was a mission; she wanted to improve the quality of people's lives through a new approach to exercise. From Puerto Rico to New Jersey, from Seattle to Atlanta, Jacki continued to spread her ideas. Exercise didn't have to be drudgery, she taught; it could also be fun. You didn't have to get down there on the floor and sweat and groan and hate every minute of it. It could be a creative experience, you could add grace along with tone, and Aerobic Dancing could be a social outlet, all at the same time.

In city after city Sorensen developed a loyal following. Because she didn't feel she would be able to control the quality of her product, Sorensen chose not to set up franchise operations across the country as, for example, Jack La Lanne had done. Instead she hired local instructors who agreed to her rules: They couldn't be smokers. They couldn't be overweight. They had to agree to maintain exemplary physical condition. By the mid-seventies, Sorensen was besieged with requests to give clinics everywhere. She accepted the ones where she could reach the most people and "change more lives." She was not only setting up a grass-roots following but she also, like La Lanne, Dr. Kenneth Cooper, and many others, was building the fitness industry in America.

And then came Jane. *Jane Fonda's Workout Book*, published in 1981, soon zoomed to the top of national best-seller charts, where it stayed for months. Suddenly aerobics was the new way to get in shape. Stuart Karl helped spread the news when he produced Fonda's *Workout* video, which sold another million. Aerobics classes started to appear everywhere. But to Sorensen's chagrin, instead of being classes, they were organized on a drop-in basis, the same routine each time. The philosophy underlying these sessions could be spelled out in two words: *the burn*. "The mentality came from the Jane Fonda explosion," Sorensen explained. "People started thinking, *Well, that's the way.*"

To Sorensen, it decidedly *wasn't* the way. Yet Fonda forced

233

upon her a supreme challenge: Either innovate or stand on the sidelines. Sorensen chose to incorporate some Fonda-inspired methods. As she explained:

> There was a need for us to have courses that would fit the life-style of people better in the 1980s, which means they're not all going to be able to commit themselves to a course. I had to do something about that. This was a tough one because how could I not change the quality—it was still going to be fun, an interesting experience, entertaining—and still make it so that you could drop in any time and we wouldn't have to stop and catch you up. So the teaching had to be built into the choreography. It was a whole new way of presenting a class. I said, "Okay, America, you want to be on the floor, then I'll take my floor segment and expand it. But I'm not going to deprive you of your aerobics. You still get at least thirty minutes of aerobics in the class."

In reaction to developments that were impossible to foresee, Sorensen decided to offer two very different programs: Aerobic Dancing and Aerobic Workout classes. It was like starting a whole new business.

Sorensen's response was that of a true innovator. Instead of being bitter and clinging to what she believed was better, she adapted herself to new perceptions. And instead of choosing to view Fonda as an actress who had exploited her celebrity, Sorensen chose to look upon Fonda as a terrific boon to the fitness industry. Fonda, after all, had motivated millions of women to don leotards and face the music. That was great for everybody. Because she unhooked her prejudices, Jacki Sorensen was able to adapt to the changes in her field. Because she realized that sometimes it is necessary to adapt new ideas, she designed a new program. It has been extremely successful.

Learn to Cope With Failure

People who never succeed condemn themselves for every new failure. Innovators know it doesn't matter how many mistakes they make, or even how many times they "fail." What matters is the concentrated attempt to learn from each failure and to improve performance the next time around.

Throughout this book we've emphasized that innovators win because they dare to take a risk. We haven't dwelt upon the tales of frustration, fear, anxiety, and incredible sacrifices that are often involved in implementing an idea. But rest assured they are there. We haven't dwelt upon them because the innovators don't like to dwell on such things. "I'd rather talk about successes," they'd say. Nevertheless, as an innovator you will almost certainly pass through a "face the heat" period, and you can expect at times to have to go it alone. But how far is too far?

Only you can say for sure. And that's why you must develop the ability to know when to "keep the faith," and when to "cut your losses." Naturally, you'll benefit from all of the information and feedback you can get at times like this. But sometimes in the thick of the battle it's hard to weigh the conflicting signals. You'll need to listen closely to your intuition. Don't confuse *determined* with *stubborn*. Maybe you really are too far ahead of the Wave. The innovators who survive failures and go on to success are the ones who adapt quickly when they discover that the way they envisioned their idea working doesn't square with reality. They have the openness to say, "Okay, the world doesn't accept the idea the way I'm putting it out there. That doesn't mean I'm going to give up, but it sure means I'm going to have to relabel it, change it, market it in a different way, or redesign the entire idea from the ground up." Here are some suggestions you can use in dealing with failure:

1. Don't make too much of your mistakes. To err is not only human, it is also essential in the Innovation Game.
2. Examine the mistake and the results honestly and objectively. Avoid blaming others. Instead, look to yourself for the improvement and the solution.
3. Analyze how and why the failure occurred. Plan and practice the necessary steps to correct the performance. Find someone who has already solved the problem. Or, if the problem is so new that no one has ever confronted it before, search for analogous problems and study how they were solved.
4. Concentrate on the lessons to be learned, not on the temporary setback.
5. Prior to trying again, clearly visualize yourself handling the situation affirmatively and correctly.
6. Take new action to turn the setback into a setup for future success.

Continue to Take Risks

Individuals, companies, even nations, can fall into the trap of resting on their laurels. They get blind-sided by change and find themselves in a *reac*tive rather than a *proac*tive mode. Nations that rest on their laurels take their success for granted. They become complacent. Eventually their productivity growth comes to a standstill. They live beyond their means, saving little and borrowing profusely to cover huge deficits. They defer their debts to the next generation.

Innovation was not crucial to America in the years after World War II because there was no "wolf at the door." Today there is: foreign competition.

The innovators we studied are aware of and deeply concerned about these issues. They do not all agree on the solutions, but each makes it a point to be part of the solution rather than part of the problem. Among them is Fred Smith and his team at Federal Express.

Why else would the company have innovated constantly since its inception in 1973? Smith's breakthrough concept was enough to launch the company, but it has taken thousands of other behind-the-scenes innovations to make "absolutely, positively overnight" a reality. After an intense "face the heat" period during which the company ran up $30 million in losses, Federal finally created the market which Smith foresaw.

But Federal didn't stop there. Instead, it listened carefully to what customers were saying—and responded with additional services. In 1976, the company responded to growing demand to move documents as well as packages. They introduced an overnight document service. In 1981, they introduced the Overnight Letter. In 1984 Federal began service to Europe and Pacific Rim countries. Jim Barksdale, Federal's chief operating officer, compares the experience of Federal Express to the evolution of the railroad industry of the 1880s:

> Imagine how many innovative things were done in trains then. "You had to figure out how to build a roundhouse, how to run a company that was so spread out, and so forth. Today, those things seem mundane. But then they were technological innovations. The successful railroads were the ones which continued to innovate. To move packages overnight against a very finite service commitment and do it reliably in the numbers we do [approaching six hundred thousand a night in 1985] *forces innovation on you or you will get run over.* For example, I know that right now we're out of cargo containers in the Northeast and we have no more in the Hub and I'm flat out of airplanes and people are working as hard as you can get people to work and the weather is closing in in Denver. And it's bad at six hundred

thousand. So then I say, what's it going to be like at a million packages? Well, you have two choices: You can either step away from the plate and let somebody else figure it out, or you can get your thinking cap on and figure it out yourself. You have got to change the way you're doing it today because the way you're doing it today, even though it's wonderful, won't work when you have a million packages a night. And if it works at a million, it won't work at two million. So growth and change demand innovation. They force it. You cannot stand still.

Federal's biggest innovation to date is ZapMail, potentially an even bigger concept than overnight express delivery. Launched in 1984, Zap enables a customer to send a copy of a document to someone in another city and have it delivered within two hours by courier, or instantly, if the sender and receiver both have ZapMailer facsimile machines in their offices. ZapMail is no minor innovation, and therefore it is no minor risk. The company knew it would need to risk as much as $1.2 billion over a decade, almost as much as it had spent on trucks, service centers, and planes for its original business. Why start ZapMail when the package business was producing such impressive annual gains? Smith answers that question this way:

Through our contact with basically every office in America, we began to understand that people really wanted to move these documents instantly. We had created a nice business for ourselves, but it was really just a compromise away from what the true demand was in the vast majority of cases. What they really wanted to do was take that piece of paper, and just as they move it to the person's desk across the hall, they wanted to be able to move it to anyone's desk, period.

Another motivating factor was what Smith refers to as Federal's "mission orientation." More than any other single factor, it was this one that motivated Smith and his team to vote for Zap. "There is within the culture of [this] organization a mission orientation, that we would like to do things that are important and that are useful to people on a fairly large scale."

ZapMail ran into major problems almost immediately. It lost $125 million in 1984, $150 million in 1985, and was expected to lose $100 million in 1986. In the 1985 annual report, Smith and Barksdale acknowledged that the financial return from Zap had been "frankly, disappointing. . . . We underestimated the time it would take for our customers to feel comfortable with ZapMail." Not only that, the company that had spent years building a reputation on reliability was suddenly having trouble meeting its delivery promises. In March 1986, the company imposed a moratorium on further marketing of Zap until these service problems could be resolved.

Is ZapMail an idea before its time? Do businesses really want to be able to transmit documents back and forth in seconds rather than using the mails or overnight letters? Where is the market? Why hasn't Federal's marketing splash made more of a difference? Even the company's top brass seem to be entertaining doubts. In our interview with Jim Barksdale, he said:

> If we had known what was going to happen during the first eighteen months between the growth, the cost, the revenue, and so forth, would we have done it anyway? The answer is, probably not. But now that we're into it, and we understand it so much better, we're starting to see our way. The problem is that most customers don't understand the similarities; they only understand the differences. It's taken a while to get people's minds to understand how this thing works and how it fits their day-to-day business.

Because Federal Express chooses to be a leader rather than a follower, this "face the heat" period may go on for a while. But it won't cause the company to give up. Instead, the company has redoubled its efforts to listen to the customer's needs.

Barksdale summarizes Federal Express's approach to innovation this way: "Don't listen to the critics, listen to the customers. The critics, being critics, will always give you the reasons an idea won't work, which are probably valid reasons. You can convince yourself that the risks are far greater than the reward, if you listen to the critics. But the more critics there are of an idea, *the more valuable the idea will be if it works.* Because that means you will have the field to yourself."

Learn to Handle Success

Remember who you are. Remember where you came from. Remember where you're going.

Harry S Truman

Why is it important to learn how to handle success at the same time you're struggling to achieve it? One answer is, *Because gaining a realistic understanding of success will help you achieve it.* And once you achieve it, you'll be better able to sustain and enjoy it. Success won't throw you off your game.

When your Breakthrough Idea catches on with a customer group, you really will ride the Wave. Then many other factors will come in and complicate your life. One of these distractions may be fame. Some innovators say handling fame is perhaps the biggest challenge of all. If you can't, you won't ride the Wave for long. You'll stop looking for new ideas. You'll stop seeking feedback. You'll start believing that you are as great as your press clippings make you out to be. You'll ignore your team. Your ego will distort your judgment. In short, you'll fall off your game.

Enough of the warnings. What can you do right now to prepare for a sustainable success? Here are some suggestions:

1. Define what success means to you. If you're like most innovators, your goal is to implement your Breakthrough Idea. But what is beyond that goal? What is more important than that goal? People who have a clearly defined goal and are obsessed with achieving it must be careful—they often reach it. But instead of satisfying, it leaves them feeling empty, burned out, directionless.

How can you avoid this trap? Visualize yourself having already achieved success. Imagine what it will be like when you achieve your goal. Then ask yourself what assumptions you are making. What is it you are really after? What kind of life are you trying to create for yourself?

We've all heard the saying that success is a journey, not a destination. It's true we can experience success only periodically. This is what keeps us fueled and wanting to continue to innovate. Don't think in terms of "When I reach a certain level then I'll truly be successful." Achieving success does not mean that you leave failure behind. As Stuart Karl remarked:

> The bigger you get, the more you've got to lose. Everybody says, "Well, you're real successful now." And I say I worry just as much today as I did before because this [success] doesn't mean anything. Failure follows success. No matter if I have a five-hundred-million-dollar company, you never know. So I never look at it like that. You've just got to keep running as if you've got not one cent and you're doing it for the fun of it.

2. Focus on where you're going, not where you've come from. We asked a number of innovators for advice about coping with the pressures of success. *Keep your head,* was one comment. Remember you were lucky. Stay close to your roots. Keep in touch with the things you know are right before your life undergoes change. Spend time with folks who keep you human, who don't see you as your image but as who you really are. Tom Peters said, "When you read your press clippings and begin to believe them, you've got real serious problems."

3. Treat failure and success the same. When we asked pioneering surgeon John Shea for his advice on how to handle success, he replied, "Treat [failure and success] both the same." Having successfully developed the stapedectomy operation at age thirty, Shea became an international celebrity in medical circles. But, as he told us, he tried "a whole bunch of things after that that didn't work as well, [and] didn't get as noticed.

"All I can say," Shea said, "is that you just have to accept that for everything you succeed in you probably have five more that you fail with. And you've got to get yourself ready for the failures that will be down the line.

"I like Tennyson's poem 'The Psalm of Life,'" he continued. "Tennyson said that there would be triumph and disaster, and that we must treat them both the same. I don't think a day goes by that I don't think of that poem. I come home and my wife and children ask me how it went and I say, 'Well, today I had to deal with triumph and disaster and I tried to treat them both the same.'"

Tennyson—and Shea—are onto something. The ability to stand apart from success and failure and examine why each occurred is one of the most difficult tasks in staying on your game.

A Final Word

The message contained in today's headlines is abundantly clear. It reads like this: "Jobless Scratch for Survival in High-Tech Era," and "Middle Managers Face Squeeze as Cutbacks and Caution Spread." It is contained in headlines such as, "Millions Bypassed as Economy Soars," and "The Sun Belt's Boom Is Over; Frost Belt Making Hay," and "A Fading Dream: Middle Class Losing Standard of Living." This list of actual headlines from major U.S. newspapers could go on and on.

It needn't. Having read this far, you have demonstrated that you do not want to become the next victim of today's tumultuous changes. You want to use change to take you where you want to go in life. Now you can.

We hope we have demonstrated in these pages that innovation is not an innate talent, or that it is a game only the elite can play. We hope we have shown you, through the examples of men and women using these principles, that it is possible to learn to be an innovator.

Take a lesson from America's new winners. Teach yourself their Secret Skills by using them every day, and you can look forward to a lifetime of winning the Innovation Game.

Notes

Chapter 1   Winners in a World of Change

                                                 Page

"They Aren't Called 'Terminals' for Nothing" appeared in the *Wall Street Journal,* April 25, 1986.   19, 20

Alvin Toffler's book is *Future Shock* (New York: Random House, 1970).   20

Structural unemployment figures are from data compiled by the U.S. Bureau of the Census in Washington.   21

Ted Peterson is a pseudonym; his story, however, is true.   21, 22

David Birch's quote on the lack of job security in large companies is from an interview with Robert B. Tucker.   23

Figures on U.S. semiconductor industry are from "High Technology Layoffs Spur Fear in California," by Robert Lindsey, *New York Times,* November 18, 1985.   25

Statistics on Americans' declining standard of living are from the U.S. Census Bureau.   25

Lester C. Thurow's quote is from "The Hidden Sting of the Trade Deficit," by Lester Thurow, *New York Times,* January 19, 1986.   25

Michael E. Porter's concerns about U.S. competitiveness are expressed in "Why U.S. Business Is Falling Behind," by Michael E. Porter, *Fortune,* April 28, 1986.   25

The Louis Harris survey on the increasing American work week was reported in Richard Phalon's column in *Creative Living,* Summer 1985.   27

Page

The Wave analogy was supplied by Rinaldo S. Brutoco.   28

The story about Fred Smith is from various sources, including interviews with Smith by Robert B. Tucker. Smith's quote, "They were so steeped in their own rules . . ." is from an interview with Smith by Bill Moyers for his 1981 PBS series, *Creativity*.   30–32

Information about Jacki Sorensen is from an interview with Robert B. Tucker.   32

Information about Marva Collins is from an interview with Robert B. Tucker.   33–35

Statistics on the impact of the VCR on the networks' share of prime-time television viewing are from "The Networks Try to Recapture Our Attention," *New York Times*, October 20, 1985.   35

Information on Stuart Karl is from an interview with Robert B. Tucker, and from "Video Prophet: Stuart Karl Is the Premier Producer of Self-Help Videos," by Richard Stayton, *Republic Scene*, October 1983.   36

Information on Dean Kamen is from an interview with Robert B. Tucker.   37, 38

William Thompson's quote is from an interview with Robert B. Tucker.   39

Chapter 2   Your Winning Strategy

Our understanding of the lack of security in organizations today was enhanced by our discussions with Robert W. McCarthy, president of Robert McCarthy and Associates, a Century City, California, outplacement firm, and with William Pilder, chairman of Mainstream Access, New York.   43

"At a recent gathering of the Tarrytown 100 . . ." letter to members of Tarrytown 100, June 20, 1984.   48

Material about Lewis Lapham is from interviews conducted by Robert B. Tucker, and from Lapham's essay "Imagination: Data-glut Cure," *Advertising Age*, February 6, 1984.   49

"Companies looking for problem solvers . . ." quote from "How to Spark New Ideas," by Sharon Nelton, *Nation's Business*, June 1985.   51

Chapter 3   An Innovation Self-Inventory

John Welch, General Electric's chairman, is quoted in "The New Breed of Strategic Planner," *Business Week*, September 17, 1984, p. 62.   54

	Page
Information on Dr. Edward DeBono from "Clear Thinking May Depend on the 'Hat' You Wear" (interview), *U.S. News and World Report*, p. 75.	97, 98
Dr. Robert Schuller's comments from *Move Ahead With Possibility Thinking*, by Robert H. Schuller (Spire Books, published by Fleming H. Revell Company, 1973), and from interview with Schuller conducted by Robert B. Tucker.	98
Robert Giaimo's comments from an interview conducted by Robert B. Tucker.	100
"Seek out people who don't hold you in awe. . . ." Richard P. Feynman's comment quoted in *Boardroom Reports,* September 1, 1985, p. 13.	100
"I didn't know anything about educational theory . . ." from *Marva Collins' Way*, by Marva Collins and Civia Tamarkin (Los Angeles: J. P. Tarcher, Inc., 1982).	101, 102
Sir Clive Sinclair's comments appeared in Edward DeBono's *Tactics: The Art and Science of Success* (Boston: Little, Brown, 1984), p. 121.	102
Dr. Donald Moine's comments are from an interview with Robert B. Tucker.	104, 105

Chapter 6 Working With Ideas

Amy Clelland's successful solution was recounted in an interview with Robert B. Tucker.	107
See "Are You Creative?" *Business Week,* September 30, 1985.	108
David Campbell's comments are from "Breaking Through With Your Ideas," by Robert B. Tucker, *Creative Living,* Summer 1986.	108
"Mostly you go down paths that lead nowhere. . . ." Lee Clow's comments appeared in "Breaking Through With Your Ideas," by Robert B. Tucker, *Creative Living,* Summer 1986.	109
Regis McKenna's comments are from an interview with Robert B. Tucker.	109–112
Bill Gore's comments are from an interview with Robert B. Tucker.	114
Wayne Silby's comments are from an interview with Robert B. Tucker.	115

Chapter 9 Building Your Breakthrough Idea

Index